THE
SEVEN
FORCES OF
SUPERNATURAL
FAITH

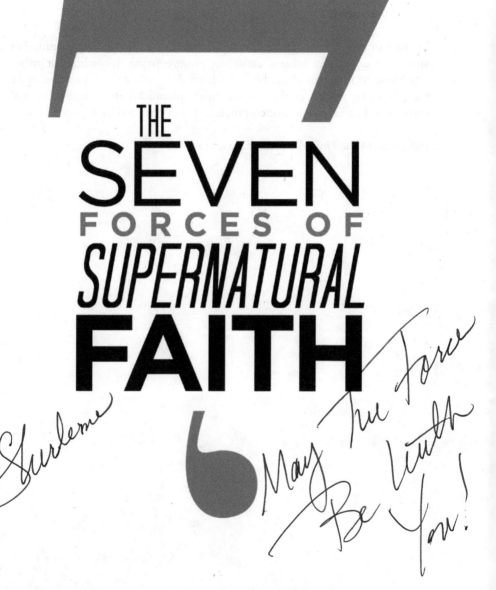

DR. SHARON NESBITT

May The Force Be With You!

Shurleme

Dr. Sharon Nesbitt

© 2019 Sharon Nesbitt

Published in the United States of America

TABLE OF CONTENTS

TABLE OF CONTENTS

INTRODUCTION

You were born believing.

Before you took your first breath, you knew how to trust God, because He taught you to believe from the womb. As He knit you together and formed your inner parts, He wove faith into the fabric of your being and made it *natural* for you to believe. Your trust in Him made it easy for you to believe others, which is why as a child, no one had to convince you to have faith. When someone told you a chair was a chair, you believed. When someone told you it was your birthday, you believed. When someone told you the woman you saw every day was your mother, you believed. No one had to persuade you to trust, because it came naturally to you.

But at some point you were introduced to an entity called doubt, which challenged what came naturally to you. Perhaps it was someone betraying your trust, parents making promises they didn't keep, or other unexpected things happening. At that point, doubt told you everything and everyone couldn't be trusted and coaxed you into a life of suspicion. Though you were still pre-dispositioned to believe God, the more you heard the voice of doubt, the harder it became to trust your Maker. Soon, you learned the art of selective faith and discovered how to believe only when it required no risk. That discovery made it almost impossible for you to operate in faith naturally and eventually shifted you into a place of unbelief. You'd still be confined to that place if we served a natural God. But we don't.

The Father, in His infinite wisdom, created a way of escape from unbelief before we ever began to doubt. He works to realign us with His original intent and teaches us how to flow in faith *supernaturally*. When we flow this way, we can believe even when trust doesn't come naturally or easily. We believe when everything around us tells us to give up or give in. We believe when manifestations seem delayed and opportunities seem expired. We stand on the Word of God when nothing seems to be happening. We obey in faith, decree in faith, pray in faith, give in faith, consecrate in faith, serve in faith, lead in faith, and overcome in faith. When challenged with adversity, we hold on to hope. We find a place in the Father's face and make a conscious decision to trust again. We don't believe from our senses; rather, we believe from our spirit through the power of God, and that makes our faith supernatural.

As we move into the supernatural, God equips us with seven forces of faith to help us attain what He's ordained for us. We'll discuss each of these forces in the chapters to come, but let's first review four endowments that accompany each force of faith. I encourage you to look for these endowments in your own life as you study this book.

- The first endowment is *supernatural strength*. When it manifests, you become strong in faith and receive the reward that comes from pushing through layers of resistance. You sever the cycles of fear that seek to siphon strength from your bloodline and learn how to impart spiritual strength to your seed. As a result, you take on such an abundant supply of strength, even your weaknesses become sources of supernatural potency.

- The second endowment is *supernatural energy*. This kind of energy is more than vitality; it's available power.[1] When it appears, you align with the frequency, fluency, and agency of faith, which enables you to operate in the power of God without self-sabotage. As you do this, your faith will rise to the same level as manifestation, and you'll cooperate with the Spirit of faith to pull resources from the supernatural into the natural. Moreover, you'll receive fresh clarity and insight about where to place the energy you've already been given.

- The third endowment is *supernatural influence*, which is the capacity to change, impact, legislate, or dominate an area to which God has called you to further His kingdom. When you receive supernatural influence, God cloaks you in a quiet but incontestable authority few anticipate and none can stop. This influence unites faith to your name (or reputation), makes you intensely purpose-driven, and brings powerful men and women to you. It unlocks pure doors that are aligned with destiny, and it's especially necessary in matters that affect multiple communities or generations.

- The last endowment is *supernatural acceleration*. Supernatural acceleration occurs when God initiates a miraculous hastening of manifestation. He expedites the materialization of what's been lodged in the spirit realm and makes you both a recipient and conduit of that release. We see a promise for this kind of acceleration in Amos 9:13 (MSG), which says, "Yes indeed, it won't be long now." GOD's Decree. "Things are going to happen so fast, your head will swim, one thing fast on the heels of the other. You won't be able to keep up. Everything will be happening at once—and everywhere you look, blessings!" That prophetic promise is as much for you today as it was for Israel 2,000 years ago, and this is the hour to see the fulfillment of God's Word. Faith is now, so there can be no more delay!

If you're ready to mobilize the seven forces of faith and experience supernatural strength, energy, influence, and acceleration, you're in the right place. In the pages that follow, you'll find principles and revelations that will rouse faith power inside of you and prepare you to accomplish supernatural exploits for our God. As you apply these principles, you'll shift from simply believing *in* the supernatural to believing *because* you're supernatural - starting with the first chapter, which will show you how to step into your supernatural self by activating faith as a creative force.

C H A P T E R 1
FAITH AS A
CREATIVE FORCE

אֱמוּן

When we study the Word of God for forces of faith, we find seven different expressions of Bible-based belief. The first comes from a Hebrew word, *emuwn*. This is the opening expression of faith in the Bible, and it means "faith", "faithful", or "truth."[2] To lay a foundation for faith as a creative force, we should closely review each of these meanings. Let's begin with the first description: Faith.

Emuwn is translated "faith" only once in the Bible – in Deuteronomy 32:20. Here, the Lord speaks of Israelites who have strayed from His command and says, "'I will hide My face from them, I will see what their end will be, for they are a perverse generation, children in whom is no faith." In Deuteronomy 32:17-18, we learn what causes Israel to lose faith: Misdirected worship and forgetfulness. The verses explain, "They sacrificed to demons, not to God, to gods they did not know, to new gods, new arrivals that your fathers did not fear. Of the Rock who begot you, you're unmindful, and have forgotten the God who fathered you." Accordingly, emuwn is the expression of faith that deals with worship and remembrance.

Your worship life is a direct reflection of your faith life, because faith leads you into worship, and worship leads you into faith. We see this principle in passages like Exodus 4:31, "And the people believed: and [...] they bowed their heads and worshipped;" John 9:38, "he said, Lord, I believe. And he worshipped him;" and Hebrews 11:21, "By faith Jacob, when he was dying, blessed both the sons of Joseph; and worshipped." Faith and worship work together to open the heavens, deliver great manifestation, and trigger a surge of divine force to instigate a new worship and higher faith in your life. The enemy understands this process, so he tries to impede it by constraining your worship. His attempts to constrain generally come in one of three ways: Excessive busyness (the time of worship gets replaced with time given to responsibilities); distractions (the time of worship is clouded with diversions that detract from God's presence); and weariness (the time of worship is half-heartedly or only moderately pursued, due to burnout or consistent strain in a single area). To circumvent these traps, guard yourself against the thoughts, patterns, settings, and people that dissuade your worship. When you feel vulnerable or overextended, take special care to avoid these entities and place yourself in environments that strengthen the worshipper in you. Gird up the loins of your mind with the Word, and reorient your life around the presence of God. This will fortify your faith, refresh your worship, and stimulate your remembrance of God.

Remembering God simply means putting Him first and honoring Him with the totality of our being. We do this by perpetually rehearsing the goodness of God and love of the Lord in ways that reveal His

2

original intent (more on this in a moment). When we fail to remember God, as the Israelites did in Deuteronomy 32, we slip into a mentality that reflects the fall of man rather than the mind of God.

The fall of man subjugated the Earth and everything in it (including humanity) to a debased level of operation and communication. Just as humankind was designed to mirror the Father, the Earth was designed to mirror heaven, and communication in heaven takes place via thought – not via spoken word. When compared to exchanges that occur by thought, the spoken word is deemed an inferior form of communication, because it requires no relationship between the speaker and recipient. In contrast, communication that happens via thought discloses a deep relationship between the speaker and recipient (if you've ever been so close to a person that you know what he or she is thinking without having to ask, you understand how this concept works). Before the fall, man walked so closely with God, words weren't necessary between the two. This is evident in passages like Genesis 2:16-17, which says, "And the LORD God commanded the man, saying, 'Of every tree of the garden you may freely eat; but of the tree of the knowledge of good and evil you shall not eat, for in the day that you eat of it you shall surely die.'" The word "saying" used in Genesis 2:16 comes from the Hebrew term *amar*, which means "to speak" or "to utter", but it can also mean "to think", "to commune", or "to say in one's heart."[3] Thus, the verse could also be translated, "And the LORD God commanded the man, *thinking*, 'Of every tree of the garden...'" Further, "amar" is the same term used throughout Genesis 1 in the phrase "And God said", which could also be

3

interpreted as "And God thought."[4] In light of that linguistic nuance, consider viewing the creation narrative in a slightly different way: God *thought* of light, and light appeared; God *thought* of seasons, and seasons were fashioned; God *thought*, "Let us make man in our image," then He created us.

God has always spoken by way of thought, and His pattern hasn't changed. That's why He knows the thoughts He thinks toward you, why His thoughts of you outnumber the grains of sand in the Earth, and why He speaks to you through your thoughts. You can hear His voice without audible words because you're in relationship with Him, and Adam had that same experience in the Garden. Before sin entered the world, Adam knew what God was saying without needing a human language. In actuality, Adam was so close to the Father, the thoughts of God *were* the thoughts of man. Only after the fall did God's thoughts became higher than man's, a change that signified a separation between the natural and supernatural realms. One of the worst consequences of this separation was humanity's aptitude to forget God and lose consciousness of His presence.

When a consciousness of God is lacking, mankind can only think of and respond to what's visible in the natural because he's functioning from a state that values sight over spirit (remember, Eve *saw* that the fruit was good). That state restricts faith from moving beyond the boundaries of visibility, which is why the Israelites in Deuteronomy 32 put faith in idols they formed and could see. But misdirected worship blinded them from seeing themselves as people made in the image of God who were capable of displaying His very being. These Israelites,

4

like many believers today, had a sight problem because they had a faith problem – but God, in His goodness, provided a remedy for both issues by pointing His people back to *emuwn*. Emuwn is the expression of faith that restores our consciousness of God and enables us to see Him at work in and among us. It lifts us into a level of mindfulness in which strategy is accessible, solution is inevitable, all things are possible, and we're unstoppable because of faith and in faithfulness (which are two other descriptions of emuwn).

Faithfulness is often perceived as dedication, consistency, and ethical dealings, and all those meanings are applicable in this discussion; however, faithfulness can also indicate a fullness of faith or profusion of belief, which suggests that diligence, constancy, and morality come out of an abundance of faith. This understanding would explain why people who have little faith in God can't remain faithful to the things or people of God; they can't operate in a faith-fullness they don't possess. In fact, faith is so central to faithfulness, instead of rendering the latter part of the statement involving emuwn in Deuteronomy 32:20 as "children in whom is no faith," some translations read, children in whom is "no faithfulness" (ESV), "no integrity" (NLT), or "no loyalty" (NET). No matter what the translation, the message is clear: Emuwn is the faith that produces staying power, and staying power undergirds the proclamation of truth that's released through the creative Word. To fathom this type of Word, we must return to Genesis 1.

Genesis 1:1-3 says, "In the beginning God created the heaven and the earth. And the earth was without form, and void; and darkness was upon the face of the deep. And the Spirit of God moved upon the face of the waters. And God said, Let there be light: and there was light." When the Spirit moved upon the waters, the word of God was emitted, and light broke into the formless, dark void. Creative power erupted when the Spirit and Word of God came into motion, and that same power was present on the day of Pentecost. After the Spirit of God moved upon the disciples and Peter proclaimed the word of the Lord, 3,000 souls were added to the kingdom and the New Testament church was created. Like Peter, we're supposed to operate in creative power by moving with the Spirit and speaking the Word. God is shaping us into agents who know how to use faith as a creative force to bring to fruition the words He's already spoken.

Jesus, who is the Word of God, is both the firstborn of all creation and source of divine creativity. Colossians 1:16 says, "For by him were all things created, that are in heaven, and that are in earth, visible and invisible, whether they be thrones, or dominions, or principalities, or powers: all things were created by him, and for him." Since Jesus is the purpose for and foundation of all existence, we can only fulfill His purpose for our lives by hearing His voice and enacting His Word. The enemy knows this, so he works hard to make us doubt and disregard the Word of the Lord (whether that Word is written, preached, or prophetic), and he's been doing this since the days of Adam and Eve. Just as he tried to deceive Eve to believe she could attain a better life by going against God's Word, so he tries to persuade believers today. By using voices that endorse paths contrary to God's direction, the enemy tries to obscure our thinking and weaken our ability to discern the right course for our lives. If we entertain these voices, we'll forfeit the creative manifestations that come only through obedience, but if we silence these voices by following God's Word and direction, we'll begin to operate in the force of faith that maximizes creative power. This force, emuwn, emboldens us to create answers where there are issues, peace where there's chaos, resources where there's deficiency, and hope where there's despair. The more we galvanize faith as a creative force, the more God transforms our voices into instruments that can advance His kingdom.

Any time we come into a new level or greater expression of faith, God will change our voice. We see this tendency throughout the Bible when there's a shift from preparation to fulfillment. Take, for example, Moses and Joshua. Both were faithful men who led the Children of Israel in truth and charged the nation to maintain proper worship and remembrance of the Lord, but Moses and Joshua had very different voices. Moses had a voice that worked in the wilderness, but Joshua's voice was pre-coded for the Promised Land. Consider how Joshua's voice was lifted in concert with Israel when the walls of Jericho fell flat; how Joshua's voice commanded Israel's army as it possessed one territory after another; how Joshua's voice made the sun stand still during the battle at Gibeon; how Joshua's voice ordered the Israelites to choose whom they would serve. Joshua's voice was connected to the fulfillment of God's promise to Israel, so as long as the Israelites obeyed his voice, they experienced great manifestation.

We see a similar shift from preparation to fulfillment in the story of John the Baptist and Jesus. John was the voice crying out in the wilderness about a soon-coming voice that would forever change the world; that voice was the voice of Jesus and fulfillment. Though John cried out for God, Jesus *spoke as* God, and the distinction between their voices teaches us an important tenet in kingdom communication. Although there are times when we're instructed to cry out, crying out isn't the end. After we cry out, we need to come out, and we should always emerge sounding like God; that means we should be saying what God says and moving in the authority of His creative Word. His Word transitions us from mourning to dancing, from sadness to joy, and from expectation to manifestation, and we receive the fullness of that Word by undergoing a mind change. Rather than focusing on previous sins and present shortcomings, we start to proclaim the presence of God in our midst. We're no longer in John's dispensation of faith, so we aren't waiting for God to come. God is here because God is in us, and in His faithful presence all things become new.

Newness is enthusing, but it challenges us to be flexible in faith. While we're grateful for the ways God has worked, provided, and moved in the past, we can't expect Him to operate in that same exact way in a new season. We have to seek the Lord to understand what would please Him now and what He wants to do in and through us in the present moment. If we cling to God (who doesn't change) and His eternal purpose, we won't be intimidated by the newness of any season or assignment. New assignments are often among the first things God distributes during a time of fulfillment, so we have to remain fluid in our willingness to serve however He sees fit. That willingness will actuate a supernatural grace that produces great effectiveness, power, and humility in our lives and ministry. The more we serve out of that grace, the less critical we'll be of ourselves and others, and the more we'll realize that we'll never be in a place to critique what God is creating, how He is moving, or who He is using. He doesn't need our permission to work, but we need His presence to exist.

Along with a new assignment, we must be sensitive to new methods. The fact that a strategy worked before doesn't guarantee that it'll work now. God is so inexhaustible, He can constantly give us strategies we've never contemplated. So, be open to fresh thoughts, ideas, and technologies as you come into something new. What sustained you in the last season won't suffice in this one, because the resources you need for anticipation are different from the ones you need for completion. Ask God to show you what He's requiring and desiring from you in this place, and search your life for signs of newness. Your praise and prayers and thoughts should be different than they were five years ago, because you should be in a new place in God – and so should those around you.

When believers in a local assembly commit to manifesting newness in worship, praise, prayer, and giving, the entire ministry will break forth in supernatural acceleration. Every person within and connected to that body of believers will be launched into a realm of expedited, exponential fulfillment that hastens the manifestation of prophetic promises. As believers in the assembly come into a fresh unity of faith, they'll take on a miraculous momentum that obliterates obstacles that used to hinder the ministry, and their alignment with God will multiply peace among one another. If they stay in this momentum long enough, they'll become a force of faith (not just employ a force of faith) God uses to advance the ministry in ways that impact generations. Their faith will become a tangible agent that magnetizes the power to possess every promise, and they'll begin to create new systems, tools, and technologies that produce a fresh economy for the ministry. In other words, their creative faith will engender a creative wealth that can be used to help fund the Kingdom of God (more on this in chapter seven).

As you position yourself to engage faith as a creative force, don't be surprised by unexpected challenges; they're simply opportunities to exercise your faith. I can recall one opportunity in particular that came when our church had a $20,000 need. I didn't want to access the general budget to meet the need, so I asked the Holy Ghost for a strategy. I didn't just pray in the Spirit out of routine; I asked the Lord how to pray (remember, methods can change.) He told me to go into our sanctuary and get on the altar. I stayed there about five minutes, then He said, "Get up and run." I asked, "Run?" "Run," He responded again. So, I got up and began to run. About 10 laps in, I inquired, "How long do I need to run?" I didn't hear an answer, and I didn't wait for one. We needed $20,000, and I needed to operate in faith with a creative strategy. I couldn't let my faith fail, and I couldn't rely on faith from an old season. Faith had to be *now*. So, I kept running. After about 20 laps, I was worn out. But I was still moving. Still obeying. Still believing. About that time, my sister came into the sanctuary and said someone was on the phone for me. I told her, "I'm in prayer," but she said, "This is an emergency, and I think you need to take the call."

Reluctantly, I consented and proceeded to the phone. On the line was the voice of a woman who was crying out. When I asked what her emergency was, she said, "For the last two hours, the Lord has been dealing with me about a little stock I need to sell so I can give you the money. It's $20,000."

Right then, I shifted from a place of expectation to fulfillment, and that's what you're getting ready to do. This is the hour for you to operate in manifestation and demonstrate faith as a creative force. To do so, you must embrace emuwn and evaluate your worship life, your ability to remember and think like God, your stewardship of faith, and your faithfulness to God's Word for your life. Ask the Lord to help you live in the newness of His Spirit, and use your voice to energize the creative power that rests on the inside of you. If you set in motion this force of faith, you'll not only see the new thing God is doing – you'll *be* it.

CHAPTER 2

FAITH AS A SUSTAINING FORCE

אֱמוּנָה

Say this aloud – El Emuwnah.

You just spoke a Hebraic name for God that means "The Faithful God". Like its root, emuwn, emuwnah means "faith", "faithful", "faithfulness", and "truth", but it also means "fidelity", "firmness", "stability", "steadiness", and a "set office."[5] Hence, when we call El Emuwnah, we speak the name of a faithful God, a firm God, a stable God, a steady God, and an official God who shows us how to embody these same characteristics by engaging faith as a sustaining force. The sustaining force preserves what the creative force of faith has produced, and we must have it to maintain faith as a lifestyle, as a revelation, and as a position. All three of these entities find their faith origin in emuwnah, so we'll refer back to that term as we study each area. Since we just learned about using faith alongside the Word, we'll begin the discussions on faith as a lifestyle, a revelation, and a position with a brief prayer to El Emuwnah.

El Emuwnah, teach me how to live by faith.

In chapter one we reviewed faith as a practice (one that involves worshipping, remembering God, changing methods, etc.), but in this chapter we'll think about faith as a supernatural lifestyle. Habakkuk 2:4 says, "the just shall live by his faith." The word "faith" used in this scripture comes from the Hebrew term *emuwnah*, and it charges believers to live out of a place of faith. To live by faith is to live in view of the eternal and intended. The eternal represents the supernatural quality of our being, and the intended signifies God's original plan for humanity. To grasp that plan, we need to reflect again on the creation event, when our Faithful God made us in His image.

Genesis 1:26-28 says, "Then God said, 'Let Us make man in Our image, according to Our likeness; let them have dominion over the fish of the sea, over the birds of the air, and over the cattle, over all the earth and over every creeping thing that creeps on the earth.' So God created man in His *own* image; in the image of God He created him; male and female He created them. Then God blessed them, and God said to them, 'Be fruitful and multiply; fill the earth and subdue it; have dominion over the fish of the sea, over the birds of the air, and over every living thing that moves on the earth.'" The first gift God offered to humanity was a blessing, which is the divine endowment of grace, favor, anointing, and supernatural empowerment given to enable mankind to serve with the capacity of God in every realm and arena in which God ordained us to operate. It's the impartation of God into mankind that empowers us to function in God-likeness. Without it, we can't manifest our supernatural structure. Only after blessing mankind

14

did God charge us to be fruitful, multiply, and replenish the Earth (tasks that require creative force), then subdue the Earth and have dominion over it (tasks that require sustaining force).

Since the first portion of Genesis 1:28 concerns creative power, which we dealt with in the previous chapter, we'll focus our attention on the latter segment of God's instruction, which pertains to subduing the Earth and having dominion over it. But what does it actually mean to have dominion? By definition, "dominion" means "to govern, prevail against reign, or rule over". It can also mean "to exert mastery or guiding influence", "to occupy a commanding position (naturally or spiritually)", or "to have control or power through legal authority".[6] When God commissioned humankind to have (maintain) dominion, He planned for us to sustain the reign of God that had just been established in and extended to the Earth realm by acting as supernatural agents who governed the Earth according to the kingdom, while living under the blessing of God. This is especially apparent given that the word "dominion" is a derivative of the term "dominio", which means "lordship".[7] Therefore, dominion was a signifier that we represented God and had been sanctioned by Him to rule. But it's impossible to sustain dominion where we haven't sustained faith. To recover the sustaining force needed to carry out God's command, we must seek a fresh encounter with El Emuwnah. He's the one who teaches us how to be just and live by faith.

Living by faith is existing in the abiding touch of God that radially changes the definitions and conditions our reality. It causes us to become aligned with and fully alive to God's purpose for mankind and prompts us to work toward that purpose now. We become ever-aware of God's active presence among us and are always seeking to demonstrate the freedom we've found in Him. Free from shame, defeat, condemnation, and unbelief, we devote our full selves to God and consistently increase in faith. Faith carries us into supernatural areas that open through dominion and helps us become a bridge that connects heaven and Earth. El Emuwnah then imparts to us the God-kind-of faith and elevates us into a faith realm that supersedes the limitations of the Earth. Through Him, we learn to process all issues with faith and view faith as the foundation of a supernatural lifestyle. We cultivate this way of life by meditating on the Word of God, focusing on the goodness of God, and maximizing opportunities that help us advance in faith as a sustaining force. As God's abiding presence undergirds our daily pursuit, we receive a sustaining power that enables us to pass every test of faith, live the life of faith, and get into the position of faith.

El Emuwnah, anchor me in faith.

The word "emuwnah" concerns faith as a lifestyle, but it also regards faith as a position. For the purpose of our dialogue, position can indicate a person's stance (e.g. physical posture or emotional disposition), or it can specify an office (e.g. a rank or assigned post). We see both meanings as we study the scriptures for emuwnah. One text in which we find this description is Exodus 17:12, which says, "But Moses' hands were heavy; and they took a stone, and put it under him, and he sat thereon; and Aaron and Hur stayed up his hands, the one on the one side, and the other on the other side; and his hands were

16

steady until the going down of the sun." In this verse, Emuwnah is translated as "steady" because it's the force of faith that brings firmness and stability. It doesn't waver, and it won't quit. It manifests when the people closest to us exhibit steadfastness in faith and discern when our hands are getting heavy. El Emuwnah sends them to remind us that we aren't believing alone and to act as pillars of strategic support who help us stay postured to hear God, for we must hear afresh to sustain all that He's entrusted to us. Their presence brings strength and energy, and God uses it to aid us in securing the victories He's already provided. Triumph and acceleration always result when people are in the right positions.

The position of faith can also speak to an office or designated post. We find this depiction in 1 Chronicles 9:26, which says, "For these Levites, the four chief porters, were in their set office, and were over the chambers and treasuries of the house of God." "Emuwnah" is the word used for "office" in this scripture, and it calls our attention to faith as an appointed place of service from which every believer is ordained to function. Faith is a supernatural service that requires us to live according to our position in the Spirit rather than our conditions in the natural, and it constantly challenges us to manifest the kingdom. The kingdom of God should be increasing within us every day because it grows every time we yield to it. Every act of intimacy with God and obedience to God is an undertaking of advancement that beckons His kingdom to come in its fullness. To further ascertain this point, we should study the word "come" in Matthew 6:10, when Jesus prays, "thy kingdom come."

In this scripture, the term "come" appears in the Greek aorist subjunctive tense, which is used as an imperative. That tense forbids any action that's not already in progress from taking place. And the actions that are in progress are only permitted to continue if they've been initiated, meaning no actions can occur responsively or by happenstance. When we view this tense in light of the text, "thy kingdom come," we realize God's kingdom won't come unless it's sought out. Mankind has to initiate an invitation for the kingdom to manifest, and Jesus taught us how to extend that invitation through prayer. Prayer instigates kingdom progress, and we have a duty to sustain prayer. In other words, progress will cease if our prayers do. That's why the Bible instructs us to seek the kingdom of God first (Matt. 6:33). The kingdom will keep coming if we keep seeking, and the more we seek and receive God's kingdom, the more we'll be transformed. We move away from the center of our worlds and reposition God as the center of our lives. This movement not only enables us to sustain Christ-centered, kingdom-driven lives of faith, it also helps us prevent personal snares in our faith walk. When we occupy the position of faith, we regularly assess our faith walk by asking questions like "Am I growing?" "Is there any sign of increase on my life?" "Do I think more about myself than I do about God?" "Does God retain the right to decide my actions, or do I try to usurp His authority?" "Am I in the same place of faith today that I was this time last year? Last month? Last week?" The way we answer questions like these will show us where we are in faith and how much work we have to do portray our Faithful God rightfully.

El Emuwnah, show me who You are.

The study of emuwnah deepens our awareness of faith as a lifestyle and position, but it's most beneficial as a revelation of God's nature. At the root of our faith is a firm conviction that God is faithful, God is good, and God is love. Absent of these three convictions, our faith would prove hollow and unsustainable, but with them it becomes a force to be reckoned with. Let's take a moment to muse on God's faithfulness.

Lamentations 3:22-23 says, "It is of the LORD's mercies that we are not consumed, because his compassions fail not. They are new every morning: great is thy faithfulness." You may have already realized "emuwnah" is the word used for "faithfulness" in this passage and noticed how it deals specifically with God's faithfulness instead of man's. While other facets of emuwnah can speak to people's association with faith (e.g. steady faith, positional faith, etc.), this description provides a clear expression of God's nature. So embedded are faith and faithfulness in the character of El Emuwnah that He remains faithful even when we aren't because He can't deny Himself. In fact, faithfulness is the standard to which He holds Himself. To Him, faithfulness is much more than devotion; it's His personal commitment to keep covenant with us (Deut. 7:9); to preserve us (Mal. 3:6); to establish us (2 Thess. 3:3); to deliver us (2 Tim. 2:13); to answer us (Ps. 143:1); to sanctify us (1 Thess. 5:23-24); and to love us (Ps. 86:15). Lastly, it's His commitment to forgive us. First John 1:9 says, "if we confess our sins, he is faithful and just to forgive us our sins, and to cleanse us from all unrighteousness." In God's eyes, to be faithful is to forgive (which means unforgiveness is actually a sign of *faithlessness*). God teaches us how to be a faithful people by being a faithful God and refusing to lower the supernatural standard of faithfulness that helps keep us alive. He continues to affirm His faithfulness to us in verses like Psalm 89:33, saying, "I won't remove from him my steadfast love or be false to my faithfulness (ESV)."

Throughout the scriptures – and our lives – God reveals faithfulness as an essential aspect of His character to help us understand who He is. Knowing and understanding His person is our eternal, inexhaustible quest and privilege, but it begins by grasping fundamental aspects of His nature. The first is that God is good. This statement is not just a saying used in religious circles; it's a supernatural declaration of God's very being. The goodness of God is reiterated time and again in the Bible. That's why the psalmist repeats, "Give thanks to the Lord, for he is good" (Ps. 106:1); why the prophet Nahum says, "The Lord is good" (Nah. 1:7); why David says, "Taste and see that the Lord is good" (Ps. 34:8); why Jesus says, "None is good but God alone" (Lk. 18:19); and why Paul says, "The goodness of God leads to repentance" (Rom. 2:4). It's the reason everything God created was good, every good and perfect gift comes from the Lord, and God will withhold no good thing from us. It's why the Father allowed all His goodness (glory) to pass before Moses, why Jesus went about doing good and healing all those oppressed by the devil, and why one of the fruits of the Spirit is goodness. And yet despite the fact that the Bible comprehensively emphasizes God's goodness, one of the chief ways the enemy works is by planting doubts that oppose the goodness of God (this is what he did to Eve, as we noted in chapter one). Often, this is how he works:

When we undergo painful situations and circumstances, the enemy tries to make us believe God is *not* good, because he knows when we doubt the goodness of God, we surrender the faith needed to manifest anything good (anything like God). So, when we face seasons that try our faith and integrity, it's essential for us to confess three things constantly: *God is faithful. God is good. God is love.* By decreeing these eternal truths, we begin to mute the lies of the enemy, uproot the doubt that jeopardizes manifestation, and position ourselves to experience and receive God's character in a deeper way. The more we receive His character, the more we mirror His love.

The Bible teaches that faith works by love (Gal. 5:6). Love is the essence of God's being, so it's the groundwork of both His goodness and faithfulness. And as those made in His image, we must understand that our love capacity determines our capacity for goodness and faithfulness. We grow in faith by increasing in love, and love development begins with an understanding of God's nature. It's God who shows us how to love and how to live loved. We see this in Galatians 2:20, which says, "I am crucified with Christ: nevertheless I live; yet not I, but Christ liveth in me: and the life which I now live in the flesh I live by the *faith* of the Son of God, who *loved* me, and gave himself for me (emphasis added)." Many versions translate the latter portion of this verse, "I live by the faith *in* the Son of God" rather than "*of* the Son of God," but in actuality, the word "of" offers a more illuminated depiction of this declarative. In this verse, the Greek translation of the word "in" means, "in the person, nature, or thought of"; thus, the term "in" denotes a position of faith, meaning Paul is capable of believing only through and because of Jesus. That means the apostle's faith comes from the person, nature, and thoughts of God. So, the text isn't emphasizing Jesus as the object of Paul's faith, as if to say he simply chose to designate the Son of God as the recipient of his belief. If that were the case, Paul could revert from believing in Jesus to believing in the law or any other entity. Rather, what Paul is conveying in Galatians 2:20 is that his life is sustained only because the faith that stems from Jesus's person, nature, and mind is actively at work in him. *That's supernatural faith.* Supernatural faith stations itself in the character and thoughts of God so it can't be contaminated by doubt or encumbered by human agency. It's not a lazy faith that waits for God to believe through a person; on the contrary, it's an aggressive, yet established faith that originates in God and operates in those who know Him. And with supernatural faith always comes supernatural love, for the same God who empowers us to believe is the One who enables us to be loved.

Love is one of the few explanations of God's being that we see in the Word. While the Bible does list many attributes of God's nature (e.g. that He's patient, kind, forgiving, just, etc.), it uses the term "love" to describe His very spirit (this explains why love is the first fruit of the Spirit mentioned in Galatians 5). Love is the basis from which every work, gift, calling, and manifestation of God proceeds, so it must be the center of our faith and lives. Love prospers the work of faith and ensures that our labor is not in vain. It partners with abundant trust and allows us to flourish in all areas of commitment. It dismantles fear, incapacitates unbelief, and expels condemnation so we can live by faith and experience it as a sustaining force. Love leads us as we seek to fulfill our dominion mandate in ways that expand God's kingdom and edify God's people.[8] It imputes a stabilizing strength that rescues us when we're weak and weary, and it's as consistent as God Himself. It's our footing in the word, our address in God, and the only way to manifest emuwnah in our daily lives. For that reason, El Emuwnah is making Himself known to us in this season like never before and teaching us how to live by faith and love by faith in ways that produce perpetual victory. We'll keep victory in mind as we transition into chapter three, where we'll find love is the only power capable of sustaining faith as a fighting force.

CHAPTER 3

FAITH AS A FIGHTING FORCE

אָמֵן

You may already know some fighting words, but I'd like you to add this one to your list: Aman. It's a Hebrew term that means "to believe", "to trust", "to be faithful", "to support", "to be nurtured", "to be sure", or "to be established".[9] It's the third force of faith, and it teaches us how to fight the good fight of faith supernaturally. It also helps us realize some of the ways God uses faith to fight for us.

Aman is one type of faith the Bible ascribes to many of the patriarchs, and it manifests as relentless belief and perpetual dependence on God. We see aman in Abraham's life in Genesis 15:6, which says, "And he *believed* in the LORD; and he counted it to him for righteousness;" in David's life in Psalm 27:13, when the king declared, "I had fainted, unless I had *believed* to see the goodness of the LORD in the land of the living;" in the lives of the children of Israel in Exodus 14:31, which recounts, "And Israel saw that great work which the LORD did upon the Egyptians: and the people feared the LORD, and *believed* the LORD, and his servant Moses." In all of these scriptures, "aman" is translated as "believe", and it's so important to the life of faith that the lack of it can keep believers out of fulfillment. That's exactly what happened to Moses in Numbers 20:12, when he failed to believe God and chose to depend on himself. The text says, "Then the LORD spoke to Moses and Aaron, 'Because you did not believe (aman) Me, to hallow Me in the eyes of the children of Israel, therefore you shall not bring this assembly into the land which I have given them.'" Moses' story reminds us that God has not called us to believe one time; rather, we have to *keep* believing. Belief unites our work with prophetic fulfillment, but to see manifestation, we must contend for the faith. In the next section, we'll discuss a few contending strategies by studying the trial of Job, a man whose faith was tested in inconceivable ways.

STRATEGY 1 – PRAY IN THE SPIRIT

Job 1:6 says, "And there came the day sons of God came to present themselves before the Lord, and Satan came also among them." As you aim to contend for the faith, remember that the enemy can ascend just like you can. He's privy to your prayers if you're not praying in the Spirit, and when he knows the direction of your petitions, he'll attempt to hinder them before they have an opportunity to materialize. He does this knowing that delayed fulfillment causes many believers to fall into complacency. *But you won't be one of them.* The first way you can contend for the faith is to pray in the Spirit. Praying in a language the enemy can't understand will spare you from needless battles and protect the atmosphere of faith you're supposed to carry everywhere you go. Even if the environment is dreadful before you arrive, it'll become an atmosphere of faith when you show up because of the resident power that dwells within you. That power is greater than any other in the Earth, and it can annihilate every plan of the enemy. Cultivate that power in prayer instead of expecting God to do everything for you. This is *your* moment to contend.

STRATEGY 2 – KNOW THE ENEMY'S LOCATION

In Job 1:7, the Lord asked Satan, "From where do you come?" Satan answered the LORD, and said, "From going to and fro on the earth, and from walking back and forth on it." Notice that Satan said he'd been walking *in the earth*, not in hell. Though many people believe Satan abides in hell, he's actually still in the Earth. God hasn't resigned him to hell yet (this is why the Bible calls Satan the prince of the air). In light of that point of clarity, we shouldn't speak phrases to the enemy like, "I send you back to the pits of hell." Saying things like this proves to him that we aren't prepared to contend, because we don't even know where our enemy is – and if we don't know where our enemy is, we'll never know how he's coming.

STRATEGY 3 – KNOW THE ENEMY'S TACTICS

The Bible admonishes us not to be ignorant of Satan's devices, and when we study Job 1:8-10, we see one of those tactics in play. The passage says, "Then the LORD said to Satan, 'Have you considered My servant Job, that there is none like him on the earth, a blameless and upright man, one who fears God and shuns evil?' So Satan answered the LORD and said, 'Does Job fear God for nothing? Have You not made a hedge around him, around his household, and around all that he has on every side?'" After God recommends Job for testing, Satan poses questions to the Lord that undermine His recommendation – *Does Job fear God for nothing?* This is one of the enemy's most frequent strategies: Planting questions that challenge the Word God has spoken. As we've referenced in preceding chapters, Satan works this way with Eve. Think of what he says to her in Genesis 3:1, "Has God indeed said, 'You shall not eat of every tree of the garden'?"

When you make a decision to contend for the faith in any area, be mindful of the questions you entertain – whether they come as thoughts or through people. Don't allow yourself to ruminate on thoughts that result in doubt, and don't lend your ear to people who have little or no faith. When a doubtful thought comes to mind, dismiss it immediately with a vocal declaration of the Word. For example, if a thought like, *What if God doesn't come through?* crosses your mind, you can reject it by saying something like, "God is not a man that He should lie. If He spoke it, He'll do it! If He said it, He'll make it good!" As you speak the Word of God, you'll displace unbelief and strengthen your heart in faith. The enemy will stop asking so many questions if he knows you have answers.

STRATEGY 4 – PRIORITIZE

In Job 1:11-12, Satan asserts that Job will curse the Lord if God removes the hedge that's been placed around him. God responds by saying, "Behold, all that he has is in your power; only do not lay a hand on his person." And just like that, Satan is given access to everything

28

in Job's possession, but what he can't touch is Job's spirit. He can't attack the part of Job's being that looks and acts like God. In the spirit of Job dwells the character and nature of God, as well as the supernatural power, wealth, healing, and breakthrough of God. Accordingly, when you're contending for the faith, prioritize the part of you the enemy can never touch: Your inner man. Feed your spirit through the Word, prayer, fasting, and faith-filled decrees. These things will sensitize you to the voice of the Lord in a fresh way, allow you to see and shut down attacks of the enemy before they occur, and bolster you for the next realm of faith. With higher levels of faith come higher levels of testing.

STRATEGY 5 – WORSHIP

Once Satan receives permission to afflict Job, he does so in every area possible. He begins by taking every sign of Job's increase: His oxen; donkeys; sheep; camels; servants; and ultimately, his own sons and daughters. Often, when the enemy wants to frustrate your faith and restrict your worship, he'll attempt to assault your increase. He starts with money because he knows we can't serve God and mammon. If we're relying more on increase than we are on God, we'll have defeated ourselves. But if our faith is truly in God, we'll do what Job did in Job 1:20. The scripture says, "Then Job arose, tore his robe, and shaved his head; and he fell to the ground and worshipped." Advancing from the position of faith to the posture of worship, Job completely humbles himself and honors the Lord. He doesn't wait to worship until he can comprehend the purpose of the attacks. Worship is his first response because he learned to prioritize his inner man before the attack ever came. We would do well to follow his pattern in this regard. When unexpected attacks come, don't expend all your energy trying to identify the cause; instead, identify with God by worshipping Him from your spirit. Worship will permeate you with a supernatural, unexplainable faith that surpasses every faith you've ever known. In worship, you'll foster a tenacity in trust that doesn't require an explanation for suffering but always requires a new encounter with God. Worship will shift you from believing God for things to believing simply because God is God. When nothing makes sense and you worship anyway, you don't just contend for the faith – you *win*. Although restoration and manifestation come after you gain victory in your faith, when they arrive, you recognize that manifestation isn't the reward of contending; establishment is. In fact, it's one of the first methods God uses to fight for us.

Many times when we think about God fighting for us, we consider the many victories He's won. But triumph over the enemy is only one part of His arsenal. He actually spends much more time attending to us than He does to a defeated foe, especially when the battles we face are private. As He ushers us into the victory He's already won, He still chooses to fight for us by establishing us in faith, purpose, and prosperity. He then seals the victory in faith by establishing our family.

In every area where you're tested and you overcome, God establishes you in faith. He contends for you as you contend for the faith and repays your incessant belief with establishment (which is another description of aman). When He establishes you, He perfects, strengthens, and settles you in the area of faith where you've been tested. He gives you such a testimony, nothing can make you doubt Him in that area. Even if you're tested in that place again (recurring tests often come in areas connected to your calling or family), you remain steadfast and unmovable, and every time you operate from that place of faith, you abound in the work of the Lord. When people around you are tested in the area in which you've been fortified in faith, you can impart to them a seasoned strength you've received by way of suffering.

After God establishes you in faith privately, He'll establish you in purpose publicly. First Samuel 3:20 says, "And all Israel from Dan even to Beersheba knew that Samuel was established to be a prophet of the LORD." The word "established" in this verse comes from aman, and it confirms that God uses authentication to fight for us. When He affirms publicly what He's ordained privately, He's doing more than honoring us; He's producing a point of consistency in our lives to further align the natural with the supernatural. His validation is a personal gift of aman that corroborates His trust of us. If you feel God establishing you, don't waste any more time meditating on people who don't believe in your calling or support your assignment. God's faith far supersedes their doubt, and their skepticism will provoke Him to prosper you even more. We learn this principle from 2 Chronicles 20:20.

The verse reads, "And they rose early in the morning, and went forth into the wilderness of Tekoa: and as they went forth, Jehoshaphat stood and said, Hear me, O Judah, and ye inhabitants of Jerusalem;

Believe in the LORD your God, so shall ye be established; believe his prophets, so shall ye prosper."[10] God uses Judah's collective faith to establish and prosper the nation in a time when they face utter annihilation. The Lord will surely contend for them, but this fight will be structured as a partnership. God will defeat the enemy if the people can defeat their doubt. In other words, both parties must put aman to use. God will fulfill His Word to establish and prosper Judah, but first all of Judah must believe that Word. Not just the king and leaders. Not just the commanders and officials. Everyone has to believe, because corporate manifestation requires collective faith. When Judah unites in faith around the Word of the Lord, God supernaturally releases prosperity to the entire nation, then makes the enemy pick up the tab.

Remember the psalmist we mentioned at the beginning of this chapter who believed he would see the goodness of God in the land of the living? Well, he also believed he would see the goodness of God in his own house. After the Lord promised to establish David's house forever, the man of God prays in 1 Chronicles 17:23, "And now, O LORD, the word which You have spoken concerning Your servant and concerning his house, let it be established forever, and do as You have said." God honors David's prayer and empowers Solomon to build the most extravagant place of worship ever constructed in the Earth. As Solomon dedicates the temple to the Lord, he prays, "You have kept what You promised Your servant David my father; You have both spoken with Your mouth and fulfilled it with Your hand, as it is this day." (2 Chron. 6:15) The Lord fulfills his promise to David not only by establishing Solomon on the throne, but also by establishing the

Word in Solomon. God settles in Solomon the very Word He promised to David by allowing Solomon to be the answer to David's prayer. David asked (in prayer), Solomon answered (in manifestation), and God established the kingdom in both their hands. Simply put, He fought for their family.

And He's fighting for yours, too. If you've felt the enemy come against you and your seed, make sure you're in the right fight. You're supposed to fight for faith; you're not supposed to fight your family. Tension in the family is a diversion the enemy uses to keep you from being established. He's not really concerned with the manifestations you're seeking; what he really wants is your lineage. You should say right now, "He can't have it!" The enemy uses fake fights *within* your house to hinder you from fighting *for* your house. But here's the good news. When you've been too exhausted to fight for your family, God has never grown tired. Did you not know? Have you not heard? The everlasting God, the LORD, The Creator of the ends of the Earth neither faints nor is weary. His understanding is unsearchable. He gives power to the weak, and to those who have no might, He increases strength.

He's strengthening you and your legacy right now by the power of His Spirit. He's visiting your seed and establishing your house. His blessing is on your family, and no man can take it away. So in this season, you must teach your seed how to walk in that blessing, and you can begin in prayer. Find one thing to believe God for, share it with your seed, and ask them to believe with you. Release a point of agreement in your house that pivots on faith and bless your children

33

afresh. Then let God have His way. When you do this, He'll bring your lineage into a familial unity that breaks generational cycles and attracts generational blessings. And while God is working in your family, He'll also be ministering specifically to you.

Often, when God is seeking to establish us in aman, He attends a great deal to the family unit, and though He just encouraged you as a parent, He now wants to nurture you as a child of His. You may remember that the term "aman" also means "to nurture" or "to nourish", and both of these meanings unveil the last manner by which God fights for us: Parenting. He fathers us. He mothers us. He cares for us in ways that keep us from attracting attacks directed to believers who carry an orphan spirit. Sometimes He nurtures us directly, and other times He uses people as an extension of His care. We see this throughout the Bible in verses that relate aman to nurturing. For example, God uses Mordecai to do it for Esther in Esther 2:7, "And Mordecai had brought up Hadassah, that is, Esther, his uncle's daughter, for she had neither father nor mother." He uses Naomi to do it for Obed in Ruth 4:16; "Then Naomi took the child and laid him on her bosom, and became a nurse to him." He even uses kings to do it for us; Isaiah 49:23 says, "Kings shall be your foster fathers, and their queens your nursing mothers." By parenting us, God gives us something we can't give ourselves, and we'd be strengthened if we looked for that gift in our own lives. So from now on, pay attention to the people in your sphere who constantly demonstrate care for you; God sends them to nurture you. Be thankful for those who always encourage, pray for, and believe with you; God sends them to assure

34

you. Take note of the people who sacrifice so you can focus on your divine purpose; God sends them to nourish you. Appreciate the people who stand with you in the worst of times; God sends them to comfort you. You may not know it, but He's used people all your life to nurture and fight for you. Now is a good time to thank Him for that.

When you finish thanking your faithful Father, ask Him to help you walk in aman as you contend for the faith. Use the strategies we discussed at the beginning of this chapter and watch the Lord establish you and your seed. Hold fast to relentless faith and never tire of depending on God. You're here because He's fighting for you, and for everything He placed inside of you. Honor His effort. Rise in faith, increase in thanksgiving, advance in calling, and mature in love. Be the supernatural person of faith He's developed you to be.

FAITH AS A
MATURING FORCE

אֱמַן

Allow me to reintroduce aman. You became well-acquainted with this force of faith in the previous chapter, but that was in the Hebrew language. In this chapter, I want to show you what "aman" means in Aramaic. Although these languages share some similarities, in Aramaic the term "aman" has a slightly different connotation than it does in Hebrew. This variation isn't so much because of its description; it means "confirm," "support," "trust," "believe," "faithful," and "sure." Rather, the distinction arises because of its placement. The Aramaic form of "aman" appears only three times in the Bible, and all of those instances are found in the book of Daniel. Over the next few pages, we'll study Daniel's life to find ways to activate faith as a maturing force, but first I want to discuss faith as a person, not just a power.

Before we can operate consistently in the supernatural, we must mature in faith. When we think about creation, we see that God intended things to develop from one state to another. A seed becomes a harvest, a word becomes a reality, a family becomes a nation, a baby becomes a man. At some point, everything should reach a point of maturation that enables it to fulfill its ultimate purpose – including faith. One way to grasp this process of maturation is to personify faith. If faith were an infant, it would be uncontaminated, but totally dependent on others to keep it alive. If it grew into a man, it would be fully developed, stable, strong, and yet still able to increase. Even when it's mature, our faith should be perpetually increasing, just like our understanding of God, and the Lord knows how to ensure that we keep developing in faith. This truth is evident in His response to the prophet Daniel. Because the book of Daniel traces the prophet's life from his teenage years throughout adulthood, it provides an uncanny view of his faith maturation process. If we study it closely, we'll unearth a wealth of principles on how to foster supernatural faith. Let's open with five principles that lead us toward faith, then we'll examine a few additional tenets in relationship to the three verses in Daniel that include aman as an Aramaic term.

PRINCIPLE 1 – FIND A PURPOSE UNTIL YOU KNOW YOUR PURPOSE.

Daniel's story begins with the besiegement of Judah. He, like many other Israelites, is taken to Babylon to learn and serve that nation. When he gets invited to the royal table, Daniel purposes in his heart not to defile himself with the king's food. He's still a very young man who doesn't yet know God's purpose for allowing him to be in Babylon, but he finds something to purpose in his heart that will keep him rooted in faith while he's in a strange land. In the same manner, when you come into a season or situation where God's purpose seems unclear, make a fresh commitment in an area of faith and stick to it; it may trigger a gradual unfolding of God's purpose. Just be aware that any area in which you purpose to commit is subject to testing. Daniel actually invites this testing by asking the chief of the eunuchs to compare his countenance and that of the three Hebrew boys to those who partake of the king's sustenance. When he flourishes in this small area of testing, Daniel begins to increase in faith.

PRINCIPLE 2 – LOOK FOR ADVANCEMENT.

After Daniel and the three Hebrew boys overcome the first test of faith, God gives them wisdom and skill, and He gives Daniel understanding in visions and dreams. These four men excel their counterparts by far and are chosen to stand before the king; in other words, the gifts God has given them result in new access. One way to see if you're progressing in faith is to look for proof of advancement *during* a faith test. Development amidst a trial is always a sign of faith maturation. Any time God allows you to be tested, He wants to cultivate something new in you, and part of your responsibility is to find out what that is.

PRINCIPLE 3 – DON'T TAKE IT PERSONALLY.

All seems to be going well for Daniel when the bottom drops out. The Babylonian wise men come to him and explain that Nebuchadnezzar has had a dream and wants the wise men to tell that dream, then interpret it. When no one in the province can fulfill his request, the king makes a rash decision to kill all the wise men – including Daniel and his three brethren. Daniel finds himself in jeopardy, not because he's done something wrong, but because he's a wise man. He's slated to suffer simply because of his position. However, when he realizes the detriment of the situation, he doesn't try to defend himself or explain why he shouldn't be held liable; instead, he requests a short reprieve and uses that time to pray to God (more on this next). You can be sure your faith is maturing when you respond rightly to tests that come merely because of your position. Rather than taking these trials personally, stay positioned in faith and pure in heart so you can hear what God is saying. The answer you need is in His Word, not in your feelings.

PRINCIPLE 4 – PRAY.

This principle may seem repetitious from chapter three, but it's not. Prayer is the bedrock of the believer's life, and it's paramount in times of testing. Daniel enters into prayer with Shadrach, Meshach, and Abednego, the three men who had been tested and victorious with him in faith before, the three men who could hold their own in faith because they were accustomed to living by it. Together, the four begin to appeal to God's mercy. They ask the Lord to reveal the king's dream to Daniel so the lives of all the wise men (not just theirs), would be spared. Modeling *aman* like Judah did in 2 Chronicles 20:20, these Judahites activate a collective faith for the sake of the community by praying and believing the same thing. While in prayer, Daniel and his colleagues give no time to whining, complaining, or the accommodation of fear. They demonstrate mature faith by praying as a family of believers who need God to show His power in a crisis

40

situation, and when they realize their prayers have availed much, the men bless the Lord. Through this experience, they teach us three maturation principles. The first is to cultivate an effective, continual prayer life. Faith will crumble without it. The second is to pray with a community of believers when an issue has the potential to decimate a community of people. Some answers only come through a unity in prayer, and those who are mature in faith know when they need reinforcement. Lastly, we learn to pray with people who believe God. If the people you're praying with petition God for one thing but are actually expecting something opposite, they'll project unbelief and can block the manifestation for which the community is praying. If no physical community is accessible, pray on your own in the Spirit.

PRINCIPLE 5 – GET IN ORDER. AND STAY THERE.

After Daniel receives the dream and interpretation from God, he goes to the captain of the guard and asks permission to go before the king. Daniel has gained access to the king as one chosen to stand before him; he's distinguished, favored, and he has the answer the king has requested, but he chooses not to go before the king on his own. He follows protocol and waits to be invited in. No assumptions. No entitlement. No attempts to claim that his gift warrants an exception to the system; instead, a simple bid to speak to the king. When he stands before the king, Daniel continues in the spirit of order by crediting God alone for the revelation of Nebuchadnezzar's dream. His commitment to order provokes faith by challenging the king to focus on God. If you desire to mature in faith, one of the greatest ways to do so is by operating in order. Walk in humility and never seek to use your anointing as leverage for access. Your anointing is great, but it's not greater than order. Because God established order in the Spirit, it's expected of you to observe it in the natural. Exalt Him. Honor leadership. Observe rank and file. If you can be faithful enough to mature, God won't just shift into aman; He'll solidify you in it.

As we move into the part of our discussion that directly involves the Aramaic expression of aman, we'll see how the maturation of Daniel's faith outlined in the previous section enables the prophet to maintain an attitude of trust during the apex of testing. We'll begin by reviewing the first verse in Daniel that includes the term "aman" for additional maturation principles.

PRINCIPLE 6 – CULTIVATE YOUR RELATIONSHIP, NOT JUST YOUR GIFT.

As Daniel closes his recitation and interpretation of the king's dream, he says to Nebuchadnezzar, "Inasmuch as you saw that the stone was cut out of the mountain without hands, and that it broke in pieces the iron, the bronze, the clay, the silver, and the gold—the great God has made known to the king what will come to pass after this. The dream is certain, and its interpretation is *sure* (Dan. 2:45)." Daniel uses the term "aman" to confirm that the interpretation is sure. This is striking because there is no record of him ever using the gift of interpretation before being called on to stand before the king. It seems Daniel recognized his newfound ability to understand visions and dreams in chapter one, but the Bible never says he actually used that ability prior to this point. This suggests he doesn't share the gift publicly until the leader has need of it (notice the king never considers Daniel as one who might be able to interpret his dream). Daniel doesn't go around Babylon promoting his gift to advance his name or distinguish himself from others; rather, he cultivates the gift by cultivating his relationship with the Giver, and that relationship allows him to respond when the king has a need. Daniel is confident the interpretation is sure because he's been with God long enough to know when God is speaking. He can't rely on his skill or experience in this matter, but he can rely on God, and the maturation of his faith over the years has taught him exactly how to do that. Where Daniel is unsure of himself, he is wholly confident in God - and that's mature faith. As you continue to mature in faith, follow Daniel's example and focus more on your relationship with God than on the exhibition of your gift. The faith you develop in God will ground your gift in something greater than you, and it'll teach you when and how to use that gift in ways that assist your leader and minister to God's people. It'll also generate in you an unshakeable confidence that empowers you to minister with holy boldness and incites faith in all who are around you.

PRINCIPLE 7 – COMMIT AND SUBMIT.

When we remember Daniel's story from chapter one, we can see his faith is present and active, but not mature. Daniel commits to something in faith he already practices in life (not eating the foods of Babylon), and while this does offer him a way to build faith, it's not a sign of fully developed faith. Still, the Lord acknowledges his effort to

43

live by faith and grants Daniel distinction among his peers, as well as the gift of interpretation. As Daniel grows in his relationship with God, so does his faith. The way he responds to crisis affirms that his faith is becoming aman, and with the development of his faith comes another level of gifting. When Daniel's faith was immature, he had only the gift of interpretation (a gift common among the wise men of that day), but as his faith matures, Daniel receives the gift of seeing and interpreting dreams (a gift no one else in the province had). As Daniel commits and submits to the process of maturation and continues to enact faith through humility, God adds layers to his gift. Daniel proves himself faithful in the stewardship of the first gift, so God makes him ruler over another one. Daniel doesn't even know God has added to his gift until he's called upon to use it, and when he does, he realizes God has lifted him into a higher place of establishment (aman). Daniel is established in purpose because God has given Him public validation, established in prosperity because he unites in prayer with a cohort of believers, and established in faith because he's welcomed the process of maturation, but now God is establishing everything Daniel releases. He's establishing Daniel's word, wisdom, gifts, reputation, insight, and leadership; in other words, God is establishing Daniel's legacy. The more Daniel allows himself to be matured in faith, the more God establishes him in the region, and the more influence he gains in the kingdom (both of Babylon and of God). Like Daniel, if you commit and submit to the faith maturation process God has designed for you, the Lord will establish what you produce (not only your seed, but also everything you put your mind and hands to), just as He's established you in purpose. He'll give you the reputation and resources needed to bring kingdom influence to every region to which He's sent you.

PRINCIPLE 8 – RULE WELL.

After Daniel finishes speaking the Word of the Lord to Nebuchadnezzar, the king confesses that Daniel's God is the God of gods, then sets Daniel over the whole province. When settled in his new position, Daniel uses his influence to ensure that Shadrach, Meshach, and Abednego, the people who prayed with him, are also promoted in the kingdom. Daniel uses his authority to advance God's kingdom by placing people in power who are committed to God and who will remain faithful as they carry out their dominion mandate. One of the best ways to determine your progress in faith maturation is to see if your position of influence helps empower others to fulfill their calling. You should steward influence in such a way that the region changes because of your presence and lives are made better because of your power. Mature faith never aims to advance only the person employing it. It functions out of a kingdom agenda and helps you remain grounded when people oppose that agenda.

PRINCIPLE 9 – STAY FAITHFUL.

Daniel has gained power, influence, and authority in the kingdom because of his faithfulness to God. But with his position of power has come a following of people who know he's honorable but still want him to fail. Daniel 6:4 says, "The governors and satraps sought to find some charge against Daniel concerning the kingdom; but they could find no charge or fault, because he was faithful (aman); nor was there any error or fault found in him." This group of people searches for ways to entrap Daniel, but his faithfulness keeps the men from ever gaining a foothold. Daniel's faithfulness is apparent in his life of prayer and fasting, but it's also evident in the way he executes his kingdom assignment. He operates in such a spirit of excellence, accountability, and reliability that even his critics attest to his faith. They realize faith is the only area in which they could come against Daniel, so they seek to turn his strength into a point of weakness. Watch for this tactic as you mature in faith. When people who lack faith and are devoid of love begin to criticize your faith and faithfulness, they're trying to convert your strength in God into a place of vulnerability. Often, their critiques are directed at your steadfastness in faith, so they try to paint faithfulness as weakness. But as God did for Daniel, He'll fight for you. You need only to remain faithful to what God's told you, showed you, and sent you to do, especially when you walk through the next test of faith. As you mature, remember that faith is built through faithfulness, cultivated through fellowship with God, and verified through testing. God has a way of turning your test into a commencement.

PRINCIPLE 10 – REMEMBER THAT FAITH IS IN YOUR GENES.

Daniel's commencement ceremony takes place in a lions' den. He ends up there after the group of insecure critics convinces King Darius to enact a law that requires misdirected worship. When Daniel refuses to observe this law, he's thrown into a den of lions. It's no coincidence that Daniel, who comes from the tribe of Judah, is placed in a lions' den. You may remember that when Israel blesses his sons in Genesis 49, he says Judah is a lion's whelp. Centuries later, one of Judah's descendants is placed in a lions' den; in other words, he's tested in a place that's related to his bloodline. Be mindful of these kinds of tests as you develop in faith. For example, if your family is known for business, it wouldn't be uncommon for your greatest tests of faith to be economic in nature. Or if your family was known for artistry or ministry, it would not be surprising to be heavily tested in the industry or church. This same principle could be said of any other field. Daniel's experience in the lions' den proves that God is strengthening him in aman, the force of faith whereby God ministers to the bloodline, but Daniel passes the test by drawing from the lineage of faith that began with Israel's grandfather, Abraham. You must do the same.

When your family is tested in an area of faith, stand in your supernatural inheritance as the seed of Abraham, who is the Father of Faith. Because you're in Abraham's lineage, like Daniel, you can access the spiritual legacy of faith and apply it to your natural family. Faith is in your bloodline, and trust is in your spiritual DNA. Remember who you are and begin to pray and decree as the seed of Abraham and an heir of the promise. As you do, you'll transfer faith from your spiritual ancestry to your biological family and activate dominion in your own house. Appropriate your faith inheritance, and teach your seed to do the same so they can receive from God everything that comes by faith. You'll experience the Lord's deliverance as you access faith, and a supernatural maturation will come to your family that causes your household to inhabit a higher reality of aman. God will respond to your family if you respond to the test with faith.

While Daniel spends time in the lions' den, he holds on to the faith that's now matured into a full-grown aman. God honors his faith and sends an angel to shut the mouths of the lions – a precursor to the way in which He's about to shut the mouths of Daniel's critics. When King Darius checks to see if Daniel is still alive, he's overjoyed to realize that the man of God has been spared. Daniel 6:23 says, "Now the king was exceedingly glad for him, and commanded that they should take Daniel up out of the den. So Daniel was taken up out of the den, and no injury whatever was found on him, because he *believed* in his God." The word "believed" in this verse comes from aman, and it connects Daniel's deliverance to his faith. As the final Aramaic use of the term "aman" in the Bible, it reminds us that faith should be as present at the end of a thing as it is at the beginning and that God brings the work of faith to completion in the lives of believers who are willing to be matured. We'll find in chapter five that these are the people He uses to transform the world.

CHAPTER 5

FAITH AS A TRANSFORMATIVE FORCE

ἐλπίς

Any time you sense things changing, know that God is preparing you for a new level of faith, and He's about to use a specific force to strengthen you in and for that transformation. That force is connected to a Greek word, *elpis*, which simply means "faith" or "hope."[11] The term indicates a jubilant and confident expectation of the good, which is why we see it in scriptures like Hebrews 3:6, which says, "we hold fast the confidence and the rejoicing of the hope firm unto the end," Romans 15:13, where Paul prays, "Now the God of hope fill you with all joy and peace in believing, that ye may abound in hope, through the power of the Holy Ghost," and Romans 5:2 and 5:5, which say, "we have access by faith into this grace wherein we stand, and rejoice in hope of the glory of God," and "hope does not disappoint us." Elpis is a transformative force that denotes the author or foundation of hope, produces resolute anticipation, and assumes completion rather than potential. In other words, it doesn't hope for what's possible; it looks for what's already done. It functions in the 'already done' realm and operates in the lives of believers who use their faith to step into the reality God has prepared for them. These believers maintain joy because they remain in a constant state of readiness. So, instead of saying things like, "I believe God will do it one day," they say, "God already did it, and today might be the day I see the full manifestation!" They resist weariness by drawing strength from joyful expectation, and every time they hope, they get stronger. Their hope is almost always tied to a spoken word, because this force of faith induces commands. We see that association in scriptures like Hebrews 10:23, which says, "Let us hold fast the *profession* of our *faith* without wavering; (for he is faithful that promised);" 1 Peter 3:15, which teaches, "But sanctify the Lord God in your hearts, and always be ready to give a *defense* to everyone who asks you a reason for the *hope* that is in you, with meekness and fear;" and 2 Corinthians 3:12, which says, "Therefore, since we have such *hope*, we use great boldness of *speech* (italics added)." When believers link faith to the spoken word, they stimulate a transformative power that changes situations, seasons, and regions for the glory of God. And sometimes that change comes in unexpected ways.

Many times when we think about exercising faith to transform a situation, we focus on ways to convert that which is void into that which is fruitful, but sometimes we're called to do the opposite. Jesus models this behavior for us in Mark 11:12-14. The passage says, "Now the next day, when they had come out from Bethany, He was hungry. And seeing from afar a fig tree having leaves, He went to see if perhaps

50

He would find something on it. When He came to it, He found nothing but leaves, for it was not the season for figs. In response Jesus said to it, 'Let no one eat fruit from you ever again.' And His disciples heard it." Now that we've read the passge, let's take a closer look at this story through the lens of transformative faith. When Jesus spots a tree with fig leaves, He approaches it in joyful expectation. Trees of this sort are common in His region, so He knows they generate leaves after (or at least while) they produce fruit. So although it's not yet the season for figs, the tree's production of leaves causes people to believe fruit is either present or starting to bud. The leaves are supposed to confirm that another cycle of maturation has been completed, but when Jesus inspects the tree, He realizes it's promised but not produced. The tree appears to have manifestation but has no evidence of maturation, so its lack of fruit becomes a mockery of faith. Jesus silences that mocking with just a few words, "Let no one eat fruit from you ever again." When He and the disciples pass by the next day, everyone notices the tree has been dried up from the roots. Then Peter, remembering the Word Jesus spoke, says, "Rabbi, look! The fig tree which You cursed has withered away." Jesus answers his proclamation with a simple reply: "Have faith in God (Mk. 11:21-22)."

Jesus could have easily commanded the tree to bear fruit, but He recognized the lack of figs wasn't an issue of timing or seasons; rather, this matter was altogether spiritual. A spirit had interrupted the cycle of growth, and if left unaddressed, it would continue to stifle the tree's ability to yield fruit. That spirit was controlling, though inconspicuous, and it had an interesting name: *Nothing.*

Nothing is a spirit that attaches itself to entities designed to produce. It aims to stunt the process of maturation to hinder the fulfillment of God's ultimate purpose, and it must be cursed. Since the spirit of nothing had fastened itself to the fig tree, the only way to stop its decimation was to kill the source to which it was attached. As long as the tree was living, the spirit of nothing would remain in the region, continue to halt the production of fruit, block the process of maturation, and thwart the tree's ability to reveal its God-given intent. Since a tree is known by its fruit, when a tree can't bear, it can't demonstrate its purpose for creation. And when something God created can't be identified, confusion enters the atmosphere.[12] To ward off confusion and the lack of manifestation, Jesus transforms the tree with a divine curse. His words extract the spirit of nothing from the land and keep the tree from yielding anything marked by that spirit – like the fig leaves that profited Him nothing. Instead of allowing the tree's lack of fruit to siphon His faith and expectation, Jesus connects faith to a Word that prevents lack from ever occurring in His locale again. We must do the same.

Often, when we come into seasons and situations that should be filled with manifestation but are plagued with emptiness, the Lord is exposing the spirit of nothing and reminding us we have the authority to curse it. We legislate and adjudicate in the Earth through words, so when we speak the Word of the Lord, we can displace the spirit of nothingness and restabilize our region as a kingdom territory. We can't allow nothingness to dwell in any area God has commanded us to dominate. If we fail to curse the spirit of nothing, nothingness will spread into other areas of our lives, and we'll begin to think and say things like, "Nothing good ever happens for me," "Nobody understands me," or "I can't do anything right." The more we focus on what seems to be absent, the more power we give to the spirit of nothing. This is exactly what happened to the widow of the prophet in 2 Kings 4. You may remember the story.

When Elijah finds out the widow of a prophet and her children are about to be sold into bondage, he asks the woman what she has in her house. She replies, "I have *nothing* in my house save a pot of oil (italics added)." The widow thinks she has nothing because the spirit of nothing has taken residence in her home. Nothing good is happening for her because she keeps confessing nothingness, and her words give the spirit of nothing a right to remain. But Elijah tells the widow to do something that goes completely against her confession. The woman is to borrow as many vessels as she can, return to her home (the place where she's experiencing nothing), pour oil into the jars, and use her faith to *produce in private*. The oil, the very thing the woman calls nothing, is actually her deliverance in disguise, but she can't ascertain its purpose until she responds in faith and obedience. Her obedience supplants the spirit of nothing with the spirit of faith and allows the woman to move into God's supernatural provision. Deliverance was always in her house, and she could have felt it sooner had it only been in her mouth.

The widow reminds us that death and life are in the power of our tongue and we'll see whatever we say. Remember, only after Jesus curses the tree and expels the spirit of nothing is He able to see something. The next day, Jesus sees the fulfillment of His Word, a manifestation far greater than the fruit He originally sought. Like Jesus and the widow, you have the power to see something in every area that's produced nothing, and you walk in that power by declaring the Word in faith. That means you have to know the Word, believe the Word, and speak the Word. You can't expect to get results if you don't do anything, because in the Spirit you don't get something for nothing; you get something *or* nothing. You have to make room for something by cursing the spirit of nothing. When that spirit departs, everything and everyone connected to it will leave as well. Then fill your mouth with fresh faith decrees and declare every day that something good will happen for you. Confessing the Word in faith will fill the emptiness with substance (faith is substance) and cultivate a supernatural vigilance that will help you detect the spirit of nothing before it has an occasion to attach to your life. So, before we delve deeper into the study of faith as a transformative force, I want to mention two ways to identify the spirit of nothing and replace it with the kind of change that yields the supernatural.

Many believers go through seasons that seem to lack manifestation, but lack isn't always due to the spirit of nothing. Sometimes the absence of fruit is simply a delay orchestrated to strengthen the believer or preserve the manifestation that's to come. One way to distinguish a season of delay from an infiltration of the spirit of nothing is to survey your life for anything that *appears* to be fruitful but leaves you feeling empty. That thing could be a job, relationship, position, mindset, or even a long-awaited opportunity. At first glance that thing will look like a sign of fruition, but if it's connected to the spirit of nothing, you'll find it nearly impossible to produce anything of worth from it – no matter how much time, energy, or effort you invest in that area. The failure to produce there occurs because the spirit of nothing saps the power to progress, though it furnishes the *look* of advancement. So, take some time to examine the fruit (progress) in your life. It should have a clear connection to the Word and faith and should draw you closer to God. If it doesn't, it's artificial fruit that's allied with the spirit of nothing. But if it does, it's authentic fruit and will remain. You should be bearing authentic fruit in every way (spiritually, physically, mentally, emotionally, financially, relationally, professionally, etc.), but know that even if an area seems to lack natural fruit, if it's producing faith, it will ultimately generate physical resources. Remember, faith is substance, and it magnetizes matter whenever it's put to use. Keep exercising faith and increasing in joyful expectation of the Father. His presence brings genuine advancement that will leave you feeling purposed and fulfilled.

Another way to determine whether or not the spirit of nothing is active is to assess things that used to produce but have now dried up. Oftentimes, when God wants to shift you into a new place, He'll cause a resource that used to sustain you to wane and will open up another. He does this to lead you into a greater place of provision and prosperity, and His leadership comes by way of a Word or direction. But if God has *not* told you to move and you're serving faithfully in the place He ordained, the resources in that area shouldn't be drying up. If they are, check for the spirit of nothing. It will be near every area where you tolerate a lack of manifestation – especially if that area is spiritual. Pay special attention to patterns of laziness, lethargy, and procrastination. All of these tendencies oppose production and accompany the spirit of nothing. If you find an unproductive area, apply transformative faith to it immediately by cursing the spirit of nothing, then make it your business to manifest there. In this way, you'll violently resist anything that accommodates regression and protect generations of production by activating supernatural hope.

Romans 4:18 says Abraham "against hope believed in hope, that he might become the father of many nations." The word "hope" in this verse is elpis, and it introduces us to a powerful concept about transformative faith. This verse is often translated juxtapositionally, meaning hope is pitted against hope to demonstrate the fervency of Abraham's faith, but a closer study of the term "elpis" reveals a different interpretation. In this scripture, "elpis" means "of that upon which any action, effect or condition rests as a basis or support."[13] In other words, the verse isn't suggesting that to 'hope against hope' means to hope in spite of – it means to hope with the strength of. So, rather than imagining hope as something Abraham must overcome with faith, view it as something his faith can rest on, like layers of a foundation placed on top of one another to ensure a strong base. With that interpretation in mind, you may see that the text is conveying that Abraham hopes against hope by *layering his belief*. Years of waiting for Isaac have caused him to produce layer upon layer of trust and joyful expectation, and he reaches a place of faith that warrants manifestation by constructing his hope. Every time God comes through, Abraham adds a layer. Every time a promise is fulfilled, he lays down more belief. Every time God makes a covenant with Abraham, he pours on more trust. Hope on top of hope. Faith on top of faith. As Abraham builds a solid foundation of faith, transformation takes place within him and touches everything around him.

To walk in transformative faith, you must do like Abraham and hope against hope. Nothing about your faith is an isolated incident. Every test of faith, every moment of manifestation, and every challenge to trust is part of a grand design to lift you into a faith dimension that brings fulfillment. Think of every time your faith has grown as a single step in a staircase. Each faith is supposed to build upon another faith to provide a means of ascension, but most believers use faith experiences like stepping stools. Perceiving each experience as a remote point of progression, they stand on faith advancements for a moment but eventually return to a base level, never connecting the experiences together to reach a new height in God. They don't realize major manifestations require layers of faith from every part of a person's being.

You're a trichotomy. You're a spirit who has a soul that lives in a body, and it's the will of God that your whole spirit, soul, and body be kept blameless until the coming of Jesus Christ (1 Thess. 5:23). Your spirit is saved, but your soul (your mind, will, emotions, and thought processes) is being saved and renewed.[14] Your soul has to undergo a constant state of renewal because it's inclined to operate according to the fallen state of man. That's why the Bible admonishes you to renew your mind (Rom. 12:2), to be renewed in the spirit of your mind, and to work out your salvation. The third part of you is your flesh/body, and it will be saved. The Bible teaches that you'll eventually receive a glorified body (1 Cor. 15:42-44; Phil. 3:20-21), but the body you currently have is not disposed toward glorification. It's prone toward gratification, so it tends to contest behaviors that don't provide immediate comfort. That's why your body tells you to go back to sleep when God wakes you up early to pray, why your body tells you to eat when God tells you to fast, and why your body tells you to sit when your spirit urges you to praise. The body has to be taught that it's not in control, and it will follow the leading of whatever part of you is most strong. If your spirit is stronger than your soul, your body will come into alignment with God's agenda and you'll walk in the dimensions to which He's called you; however, if your soul is stronger than your spirit, your body will follow the direction of your mind, will, and emotions. Thankfully, there's a way to bring all three parts of your being into divine alignment: Instead of only praying for external things, pray for the trichotomy that you are. Pray that your spirit would be made strong, your soul would bless the Lord and thirst for Him rather than the things of this world, and your body would be healthy and prosperous like your soul. Your being has to be transformed to maximize faith as a transformative force, and the Bible teaches that you can be transformed by the renewing of your mind. We'll close by recapping three ways to do that.

First, nourish your mind with truth. Study, meditate on, and confess the Word of God every day. Try to commit at least one verse to memory on a regular basis, and pray without ceasing. Make your mind produce by replacing empty thoughts with contemplations about what's true, honest, just, pure, lovely, and worthy of praise. Second, starve your mind of things that incite fear and disappointment. Don't rehearse issues, problems, struggles, or crises. Whatever you give attention to, you give authority to. If you focus on issues instead of God, you'll attract frustration and enrich expectancy for the wrong things. But if you set your heart on God, you'll foster the faith that brings manifestation. Third, build your staircase. Make a list of your faith victories (e.g. prayers answered, promises fulfilled, prophetic Words that have come to pass, family successes, and personal advancements in faith, practice, or spiritual commitment). Call to mind all the times God has performed and you've produced. Then, take note of the areas in which God has moved (healing, deliverance, salvation, wealth, promotion, etc.), and begin to integrate details of your faith victories into your prayers and confessions. This is what David did when he vowed that Goliath would be like the lion and bear he'd killed. You might say something like, "God healed me from sickness before, and I apply supernatural healing to my being right now," or "God blessed me before the foundation of the world, so I can only walk in divine wealth." When you recall victories, you activate supernatural faith and cultivate a supernatural mind. You receive fresh transformation and take on the mind of Christ, which enables you to operate effectively in the realm of the spirit.[15]

As you advance in the spirit and increase in faith, God will open your understanding and allow you to see, hear, and manifest on a level of acceleration that's beyond all you've imagined. Before you can think of a thing, it will happen, and the spirit of nothing will run from you. The tests you've overcome will shift you from hope to supernatural hope, and God will use your triumphs in faith to transform others. When you grow in faith as a transformative force, you'll graduate from simply experiencing change to becoming a change agent who moves in catalytic faith.

CHAPTER 6

FAITH AS A CATALYTIC FORCE

πιστός

In the last chapter we learned how to use faith to transform, but in this chapter we'll discover how to use it to trigger. It's time for us to access faith as a catalytic force, or a force that accelerates things and causes them to happen. This force of faith is called *pistis*, and we see its ability to prompt action in scriptures like Hebrews 11:3, which says, "Through faith we understand that the worlds were framed by the word of God, so that things which are seen were not made of things which do appear." Appearing more than any other term for faith in the Bible, "pistis" means "faith," "fidelity," or "conviction of truth," and it typically connotes a lifestyle or belief system[16] that links faith to man's relationship with God. It also indicates a holy passion birthed from trust and confidence that springs from faith.[17] The act of springing forth suggests supernatural movement or advancement, which we can see in verses like Romans 1:17, which says, "For therein is the righteousness of God revealed from faith to faith." As we continue our study, we'll highlight the connection between faith and supernatural movement to reveal its power as a catalytic force.

The movement of faith in the life of a believer works a lot like the movement of an atom in a quantum jump. In physics, a quantum jump describes a leap from one form of energy to another. Here's how it happens: A single atom is exposed to two different energies. One is called the ground state of energy, and it's the base level at which the atom rests. The other energy is called the excited state, and it lingers at the height of the atom's range. When light is introduced into that range, the atom that was resting at the ground state leaps instantaneously and randomly into the excited state. Like the confidence that springs from faith, the atom springs from one form of energy to another with no delay, interruption, or interference (no in-between). Even beyond physics, the act of springing forth is often referenced figuratively as a quantum leap. This expression signifies a major shift or significant change in position or disposition (typically one that involves great risk or requires great faith), and we see it enacted time and time again in the Bible. Acts 8 contains one such example.

When we read Acts 8, we find Philip preaching a revival and performing all sorts of miracles in Samaria. The angel of the Lord comes to him and says, "Arise and go toward the south along the road which goes down from Jerusalem to Gaza (8:26)." Philip proceeds to Gaza and observes an Ethiopian eunuch in a chariot. The Spirit of God commands Philip to catch up to the chariot, so he runs towards it. When he draws close, he hears the eunuch reading the book of Isaiah and asks the eunuch if he understands what he's reading. The eunuch admits that he doesn't understand, so Philip begins to preach to him

62

about Jesus. After Philip shares the gospel, the eunuch asks to be baptized, and when the baptism is complete, something miraculous happens. The Bible says, "Now when they came up out of the water, the Spirit of the Lord caught Philip away, so that the eunuch saw him no more; and he went on his way rejoicing. But Philip was found at Azotus (8:39-40)." The Spirit of God brings about a quantum leap on Philip's behalf and supernaturally transports him from the place of baptism to a city over 30 miles away.[18] Just as Philip experienced a miraculous shift from one location to another, so may believers of our day experience a supernatural transfer from one physical place to another. This notion may seem far-fetched to some, but the Bible records it happening on multiple different occasions (e.g. Elijah in 1 Kgs. 18:12 and 2 Kgs. 2:11; Ezekiel in Eze. 3:12-14; the man Paul knew in 2 Cor. 12:2-4, etc.). These biblical examples of a quantum leap all affirm that God can move people however He sees fit, but they also remind us that it's the Spirit of God who initiates a physical shift. Though believers can leap to a higher spiritual dimension by applying the faith principles that we'll review in this chapter, we don't seek to instigate supernatural acts that physically relocate us. None of the biblical exemplars listed above who underwent a supernatural shift sought to shift themselves to a different place; rather, they followed the leading of the Spirit of God as *He* shifted them into a new domain. In their day, and in ours, it's principal to comprehend that, when speaking of quantum leaps that involve physical repositioning, God initiates and man participates. It's vital to note this distinction, because some people attempt to originate a quantum leap by projecting themselves from one place to another through the application of spiritual powers that oppose the Spirit of God. I want to make clear that their approach is *totally unbiblical* and is not to be conflated with the supernatural work of God accomplished through the faith of which we speak. As people of faith, we move in and for God's purpose, not out of our own preferences.

When we study scriptures associated with supernatural movement, we realize every person the Spirit of God chooses to shift demonstrates extraordinary alignment with God. They all display utmost confidence in God's word and exhibit the conviction of the 'already done' realm, but they also model the prophetic clarity that rests at the height of that realm. Such clarity enables them to operate from an ascension called 'it is.' The 'it is' ascension is a state that reveals what God is currently saying and doing *as it happens*. While we understand that God functions from a place of rest and has already accomplished all of His eternal work, we also grasp that His actions are disclosed throughout time. Since we live in the Earth and the Earth is subject to time, we enact faith by discerning the will of God in the present, and we avail our lives to manifest that will without disconnect between God's intention and our actions. That kind of manifestation only occurs when every part of our being is aligned with the will, Word, and work of God.

Our spirit (inner man) always desires and aligns with the will of God. It seeks God perpetually and strives to display His present and eternal will (think of how Philip preaches the gospel in Samaria knowing it's God's will for him to make disciples). Our soul (mind, emotions, and personal will) has to come into alignment with the Word of God. When empowered with the Word, the soul comprehends how God desires to express His will in a given place or moment (recall that, while in Samaria, Philip receives a word from God to travel toward Gaza so he can enact the divine will in a new place). Finally, the body must align with the work of God. The body (or physical man) executes the current Word of the Lord, then anticipates the Word to come (note how Philip uses his body to preach, to journey to Gaza, to run to the chariot, and to baptize the eunuch). Before Philip is ever caught up by the Spirit, his entire being comes into alignment with God. That explains why God can use him so mightily to reveal the work that's already done *and* that's currently happening.

Like Philip, we can operate in expectation and action because we know what God has said and we see what He's doing. This dual understanding emerges from the application of faith as a catalytic force, and it matures faith from an aspiration or practice into a supernatural reality and habitation. Said differently, instead of simply pursuing faith, we use faith to show God's intent and utterances. As we express the rhema word of God, we accelerate from faith to faith and glory to glory. We see this happen in the life of the woman with the issue of blood.

In Matthew 9, we learn about a woman who's been plagued with an issue of blood for 12 years.[19] Having exhausted her financial resources in quest of a cure, she hears about Jesus and says within herself, "If I may but touch his garment, I shall be whole." When she touches the hem of Jesus's garment, her issue of blood ceases immediately, and Jesus feels power go out of Him. When He turns around to see who touched Him, the woman makes her objective known. Jesus responds to her by saying, "Be of good cheer, daughter; your *faith* has made you well (Matt. 9:22; italics added)." In this verse, faith is translated as "pistis", which, as we learned earlier, implies the type of conviction that springs from faith and causes things to occur. Notice that Jesus tells the woman that *her* faith has made her whole – not His power.

For 12 years, the woman had gone from one physician to another, hoping someone would heal her, but all the time she had the power to spark her own healing; she just had to ascend to a higher state of energy to do so. When the woman said within herself that she *would* (not *could*) be made whole if she touched Jesus's garment, she began to build strength to make that ascension. As she fortified that thought in her mind (her soul), she gained a new capacity to enact it with her body. Catalytic faith had to work *in* her before it could work *for* her. Soon, she rose from a ground state to an excited state and leapt into the realm of faith that had held her manifestation for the previous 12 years. Moving from possibility to assurance, she anchored her mind in a place of conviction and let her faith develop. She allowed herself to feel, think, operate, and function in a capacity that was different from her condition, and she began to concentrate on healing as a reality, and not just a desire. The woman so fixed her mind, will, and emotions in faith that she took residence in the reality of healing, and the supernatural movement of her faith triggered movement in her body and emboldened her to approach Jesus. The audacity of her decision can't be understated. The woman had a flow of blood, so she was considered unclean according to religious law, and those who were unclean were prohibited from being near others (let alone in the midst of a crowd). Unclean people were also forbidden from coming into the temple, which represented the presence of God. Nevertheless, the woman chose to risk legal repercussions to manifest the will of God in her body. She entered a throng of people and fought to get to Jesus – an act that no doubt required her to come into contact with those around her. Then, taking hold of Jesus's garment, she didn't just get into the presence of God; she touched God. Taking hold of fabric with her hand and of God with her faith, she extracted energy from Jesus and caused healing power to be released into her body supernaturally.

By using her spirit, soul, and body to enact the healing she'd already begun to occupy by faith, the woman facilitated a catalytic response in the Earth. She aligned the trichotomy of her being with the will, Word, and work of God and exhibited what He was saying and intending at that very moment. We know this because Jesus was on His way to heal Jairus's daughter, who was at the point of death. Jairus implored Jesus, "Come and lay Your hands on her, that she may be healed, and she will live (Mk. 5:23)." Jesus consented and was en route to manifest healing as the present Word of the Lord for Jairus' daughter, but the woman tapped into that same Word through alignment and became a beneficiary of it. She leapt in faith, landed in healing, and seized God's word *even though it was not directed at her!* In so doing, she galvanized faith as a catalytic force, and it made her well.

Like this woman, we have the power to utilize faith as an instrument of provocation. We don't have to wait for favorable conditions to believe, act, or shift into a higher realm of faith. We can align our being with God, move in confidence, and employ trust to reveal heaven in Earth right now. Many of us have made substantial progress in faith with our spirit man, but because we haven't included our soul and body in that progress, we've lacked the power to manifest. Or if we've advanced in spirit, soul, and body, we haven't continued to progress and have thus fallen back into a lower state of faith. In that lower state, the enemy tries to make us feel foolish for moving in faith, and he seeks to magnify deficiency to discourage us from acting in faith again. We can avoid his tactics by actuating momentum in a state of elevated faith.

Spiritual momentum regards the force or strength that's developed by faith in motion. When we leap into a higher state, we maintain footing in that place by keeping faith active and mobile, which is to say, we don't allow faith to rest. We constantly build it with our spirit, apply it to our mind, reinforce it with our speech, and feed it with the word. These actions make static faith dynamic, and they push us from strength to strength (Ps. 84:7). As a result, we excel in degrees of faith intensity and attract the energy needed to accelerate fulfillment in the natural. We generate evidence of the unseen as angels position us in a place of stability that guarantees fruition. And the longer we inhabit this place, the more aware we become of the need to image our faith.

To image faith is to construct a picture of manifestation with our mind. We do this because the human brain is designed to respond to what it sees much faster than what it hears. In fact, the brain is believed to process images 60,000 times faster than words, and one study even found that the brain can identify images seen for one-tenth of a second.[20] Since sight processing is exponentially faster than that of hearing, we have to image faith to pull manifestations from the spirit realm into the Earth, and we do that by finding or creating a concrete picture that reminds us of fulfillment. Seeing this image builds our faith and primes our thinking center. It trains our thought patterns to anticipate the performance of the supernatural and helps our mind respond in ways that reflect the things of the spirit. God gave us an imagination as a point of connection between what we see in the spirit and what we can produce in the natural, but our imagination is only as strong as our faith. If what we believe contradicts the faith images we see, we won't have the strength to manifest, and we won't expect the Spirit of God to do more than we ask or think.

So, take inventory of your vision. How do you see yourself and your situation? How do you see your children and your future? The way you perceive yourself right now is directly connected to the state you're in, and if you're not satisfied with that state, you need to change what you see and the way you see. Whether you know it or not, your general outlook on life shapes the way you perceive yourself and everything around you, and you emit a specific energy onto each entity you view. That energy is laced with attraction, so it draws the things and people to you that mirror your present outlook. This is why wealthy people attract the wealthy, why people who struggle flock to one another, and why people who are advancing associate with others doing the same. Energy is contagious and catalytic, and you want it to work toward your vision of fulfillment, not against it.

One of the first things you can do to make that happen is read and listen to the Word. As you see and hear the Word, ask the Holy Spirit to open the eyes of your understanding and help you plant something from that Word into your imagination. Next, evaluate your perception of yourself. Ask the Lord to show you any areas where you don't see yourself as He sees you, and if He reveals any places, create a fresh image to reverse your current perception. Here's an example of how to do that: If you know God sees you healthy but you've seen yourself sick, you could get a picture of something you want to do that requires a healthy body (e.g. traveling, running a marathon, doing activities with your grandchildren, etc.) and post it on your mirror or make it your screensaver so you see it every day. Or if you know God sees you wealthy but you see yourself lacking, you could do something like go to a car lot and test drive your dream vehicle. Take a friend with you and get that person to snap a photo of you in the car. It's important to see yourself in another state and get an image that steers change in the direction of God's will for your life. You have to see what God promised you to possess it. If your imagination is already full of scripture and your self-perception is healthy, check for residue from old, unproductive perceptions that could cause interference during your leap into a higher state. For instance, if you were envisioning a new house but still had the residue of an unproductive outlook, you might vacillate in faith by focusing on questions like, "How am I going to get the house?" or "Where's the money going to come from?" Let go of those inhibitions and use the image you created to help you move and manifest without hesitation. Set your focus and faith. You'll need both to see fulfillment.

After you learn to image faith, the Lord will empower you to be an image of the Word. Habakkuk 2:2 says, "I will stand my watch and set myself on the rampart, and watch to see what He will say to me, and what I will answer when I am corrected." This verse contains a spiritual principle that links sight to the Word of God. When you stand your watch, you stand at an elevation that allows you to see (not just hear) what God is saying and access a gate, door, or window. A gate is a portal, a door is an opportunity, and a window is a financial opening. Through prayer, you can discern how to prepare yourself for the next gate, door, or window, and then, as you see what God is saying, you also observe the timing at which these spaces open in the spirit. By faith, you step into those spaces with great precision, intentionality, and acceleration, and when you do, the Lord sanctions you to manifest the Word He just spoke. This causes you to become a visualization of His word and animate display of faith.

Faith is more than trusting God's Word. It's trusting the Word of God in your mouth and believing it will manifest. Now is the time for you to operate in faith and rule over everything you've wrestled with by leaping into the next level. New levels of favor, revelation, victory, prosperity, insight, ministry, health, business, and divine intimacy are waiting to be occupied, and God has given you the power to shift into them. Deposit the energy of the Word into the atmosphere with your declaration, align your whole being with the will, Word, and work of God, and create an image that resembles the leaps and bounds you're making in the spirit. Stir up faith as a catalytic force and make things happen for the kingdom. When you do, God will make sure things happen for you in the Earth.

CHAPTER 7

FAITH AS AN ECONOMIC FORCE

πιστός

The final force of faith comes from *pistos*, a Greek word that means "believe," "faithful," or "true." It's found in persons who are easily persuaded of God's Word and who trust His promises. Two factors make it distinct from other forces of faith, and the first is a strong emphasis on God's faithfulness. We see this emphasis in scriptures like 2 Timothy 2:13, which says, "If we believe not, yet he abideth faithful: he can't deny himself," 1 John 1:19, which promises, "If we confess our sins, he is faithful and just to forgive us our sins, and to cleanse us from all unrighteousness," and 1 Corinthians 1:9, which teaches, "God is faithful."[21] The Bible so heavily ties this force of faith to God that it's even used in a divine name listed in Revelation 19:11, which says, "And I saw heaven opened, and behold a white horse; and he that sat upon him was called *Faithful* and True, and in righteousness he doth judge and make war (italics added)." In addition to God's faithfulness, pistos accentuates the faithfulness of people, as evident in business dealings and the stewardship of responsibility. We note this accent in verses like Matthew 25:23, which says, "His lord said unto him, Well done, good and faithful servant; thou hast been faithful over a few things, I will make thee ruler over many things: enter thou into the joy of thy lord," 1 Corinthians 4:2, which asserts, "It is required in stewards, that a man be found faithful," and Luke 16:12, which cautions, "And if ye have not been faithful in that which is another man's, who shall give you that which is your own?" The expression of faithfulness through man's stewardship and God's character draws on many aspects of faith reviewed in previous chapters, so these two themes will guide our final discussion. We'll begin by examining God's faithfulness.

In chapter five, we discussed Abraham's faith in the promise of God, but that promise never would have come to fruition without Sarah. Hebrews 11:11 says, "By faith Sarah herself also received strength to conceive seed, and she bore a child when she was past the age, because she judged Him faithful (*pistos*) who had promised." Some versions translate this verse as "Sarah received *power* to conceive" because the term used for strength is *dunamis*, a Greek word that denotes miraculous strength or explosive, supernatural power.[22] That means Sarah became a recipient of the supernatural when she exercised her faith. But she didn't stop there. Although Sarah received the strength to conceive when she utilized her faith, she didn't bear a child until she judged God faithful. Notice that the verse says, "she bore a child when she was past the age, *because* she judged Him faithful who had promised (italics added)." Simply put, faith gave her the capacity to receive, but judging God faithful gave her the capacity to deliver. To judge God faithful, Sarah had to weigh the promise in relationship to God's character and reflect on His record from previous promises: I will make you a great nation. *Check.* I will bless you. *Check.* I will bless those who bless you. *Check.* I will curse those who curse you. *Check.* you'll be a blessing. *Check.* After reviewing God's record, Sarah couldn't deny that God had kept His word, and she had no reason to believe the promise for Isaac would be any different – even though it looked impossible. Abraham's body was sterile, and hers was as good as dead (she had no more eggs), so all hope for life and legacy seemed long gone. But when Sarah judged God faithful, the Lord gave her the egg that was ordained to connect with Abraham's seed, and the woman was able to produce life through faith. She saw fruition when she saw God rightly.

Many times, we don't see fulfillment because we don't count God faithful. Instead of stressing His truths and track record, we focus on the challenges of fulfillment or the delay in manifestation, and that focal point makes our heart incapable of or unwilling to judge God rightly. We judge with the heart because we believe with the heart (Rom. 10:10), but the heart can't form an accurate judgement of God based on feelings. It can do that only through knowledge given by the Spirit. The Holy Spirit downloads heart knowledge (or spirit knowledge) into our inner man to give us a supernatural understanding of God, and when we access that download, we begin to view every promise in light of God's faithfulness, and limitations start to fall away from our purview. Before we know it, a supernatural impartation takes place, and we gain the ability to perceive just as we've gained the strength to conceive. When this happens, we know God is about to manifest a promise embedded deep within the heart.

Every promise, like every trial, is an opportunity to search your heart and judge God faithful. As you await fulfillment, examine yourself and ask questions like, "Is there disappointment in my heart?" "Am I resentful, frustrated, or secretly angry with God?" "Am I doubting God in any area?" "Has hope deferred wearied my heart?" As you ponder questions like these, ask the Holy Spirit to minister to your heart and address the places in it that need to be healed. Your heart is a leading channel of manifestation, as well as the site of your treasure; so, many times when God begins to deal with it, He's preparing to shift your economy and faith, because faith is the currency of heaven.

Faith is the means by which business transactions are made in the spirit to affect the Earth. It enables us to navigate dimensions and seasons skillfully even when no external resources seem to be available. Faith keeps us stable, causes us to prosper, and allows us to weather storms that have caused others to shipwreck. Through it, we transfer things from heaven to Earth and make tangible that which was once visible only in the spirit. Because of it, we can be about our Father's business in the Earth.

To obtain anything from heaven, a transaction must be made by faith, and faith lives in our spirit! Accordingly, we have to operate from a spiritual dimension to make faith work, because it doesn't dwell in our flesh. Any faith that's predicated on the flesh will always and only seek to please the flesh, and that kind of faith doesn't come from God;

it comes from human knowledge. Let me explain. The more knowledge we have of an entity, the more faith we put in it. For example, people who grow up wealthy don't have much knowledge of poverty, so they don't believe in or see themselves ever being broke. Because they know so little about lack, they don't place faith or expectation in the possibility of experiencing it. Knowledge has trained them to anticipate abundance, so they hope for what they know. In the same manner, people who grow up in extreme poverty often foresee deficiency because they know so much about it. Their repeated experience with poverty and being recipients of aid can make it very difficult for them to come into a lifestyle that doesn't await outside help. Patterns of poverty have trained them to expect assistance, not abundance, so they tend to look for external entities to provide financial relief instead of taking initiative (catalytic faith) and causing change to occur on their own behalf. In this way, they differ from their wealthy counterparts, who have been taught to instigate and facilitate the manifestation of prosperity they expect to see. Those who are wealthy understand the value of time in the Earth, so they refuse to spend their days waiting on other people. They make things happen because they've become acquainted with faith, as well as with their ability to produce with it.

Still, no matter how people are raised, they can retrain themselves. If their soul (mind, will, emotions) has become contaminated with knowledge that impedes success and fulfillment, they can disconnect from the old man, allow God to make all things new, strengthen their heart and faith, and ultimately use it as the currency of heaven.

Powerful stories expressing faith as the currency of heaven are found all throughout the Bible. For instance, in Mark 2 we meet a paralyzed man who desires to be in the presence of Jesus, but because the place in which He's ministering is so full, the man can't enter or get close to Christ. But his friends, undeterred and undenied, choose to uncover the roof of the place where Jesus is preaching and work to ease the paralytic man down into His presence. Mark 2:5 says, "when Jesus saw their faith, He said to the paralytic, "Son, your sins are forgiven you." Did you catch that? Jesus saw their *faith*, not their money or status, and faith triggered a divine transaction to occur between heaven and Earth. When Jesus found faith, heaven released a miracle that corresponded with the friends' belief. This explains why Isaiah 55:1 exhorts us to come and buy without money. We're only able to acquire things without money when we use faith!

We see this principle further enacted in Matthew 9, when two blind men implore Jesus to heal them. Jesus asks if they believe He has the power to heal, and when the men confirm their faith, He touches their eyes and says, "According to your faith let it be to you." In other words, Jesus says, "Let the fulfillment of your request manifest according to what you have built into your faith." His response suggests their healing isn't based solely on Jesus's power; it's also based on the men's level of faith because they'll extract the degree of manifestation that's commensurate with their belief. The same holds true for us.

The state we're currently in reflects the value we place on faith and the position we give it in our daily lives. If we place a low value on faith, we'll settle for less than God ordained for us and will probably struggle unnecessarily. On the contrary, if we highly value faith, we'll prosper, and even if we lose everything, we'll recover it and more. If we place a premium on faith, we can place a demand on manifestation. Many of us haven't highly regarded faith because we haven't been taught it's the currency of heaven or how to use that currency to transact business in the Earth, so I want to offer a few strategies that can jumpstart your utilization of faith as an economic force.

First, understand that wealth comes from the Word of God. Psalm 119:89 teaches that the Word is forever settled in the heavens, but we must establish it in the Earth. The Earth is indicative of mankind, so this scripture is commanding us to establish the Word in our spirit man. Here are some ways to do that: Start by meditating on the Word and doing what it says. This will position you to prosper according to Joshua 1:8, which says, "this Book of the Law shall not depart from your mouth, but you shall meditate in it day and night, that you may observe to do according to all that is written in it. For then you'll make your way prosperous, and then you'll have good success." As you inundate yourself with the Word, apply it to every area of doubt or unbelief. Ruminate on the truth that *nothing is impossible*, and don't allow old thought processes to short circuit your faith. Just as bodybuilders go to the gym and lift weights to strengthen their bodies, go to the scriptures and exalt the Word to strengthen your inner man. Commit to disciplined and dedicated study of the Word to make your faith strong and sure, then align your speech with the Word so there's no contradiction between your faith and confession.

Second, ask God to increase the faith you've established. You may have realized that of all the things Jesus does in the Bible, one thing He doesn't do is give faith to people; instead, He increases the faith of believers who seek to move into the next dimension (Lk. 17:5). When God increases your faith, you'll gain new power to execute business in the heavens and Earth and begin to impart faith to others supernaturally.

Third, protect your faith. The enemy's job is to wear you out so you won't use faith to conduct business effectively in the spirit. He'll try to get you to move from a place of faith so you'll lose the legal right to employ it as a force, and he'll try to work through people and distractions. So, don't spend your faith or attention on matters that have no spiritual import or eternal significance. Coming into a new place of faith costs too much for you to yield your seat so easily.

Fourth, have faith in your faith. Be confident in what God told you, and remember that faith is your greatest asset. It's the unshakable, undeniable, irresistible power of God that enables you to do mighty exploits, and you must have it to see manifestation. So, sit down and assess what you really believe about God, and compare your faith to the supernatural demonstrations you want to see. Is your faith strong enough to be a conduit for the healings, revivals, transformations, creative miracles, and breakthroughs you desire? Said differently, if the Lord had to use your faith to bring about these things, would He find enough faith capital in you to complete those transactions? I had to ask myself these questions as I began to seek the Lord for creative miracles in our ministry. I'd been praying and believing God for miracles, and I started to build my faith by reading materials about people who walked in that level of manifestation. As I did, the Lord taught me not to focus on the severity of the need, but rather direct my faith energy into an approach that prompted miracles. I believed God could do it, but I needed to believe He could do it through me, so I worked to place bold faith on top of established faith. One day, a woman came to our ministry who had one leg that was two and a half inches shorter than the other, but I didn't allow her limp to move me. The Lord told me to lay hands on her, and when I did, I commanded the shorter leg to grow. It grew out instantaneously. It extended in that moment just like my faith had extended in that season, and I know God wants to use your faith to extend His power throughout the Earth. He's waiting on you to do business with faith to accelerate healing, deliverance, salvation, and wealth in both the Earth and your life.

For this reason, He's blessed the works of your hands. Expect the blessing, and begin to speak what God has said. Angels hearken to the voice of the Lord, and they'll respond when they hear it in your mouth. So when you rise in the morning, look at your hands and say, "Hands, you've been blessed by God. You can't bring me anything today that doesn't bless me." And if there's something in your life that doesn't reflect the blessing of the Lord, start to decree the Word over that area. As you do, pray for a fresh ability to administrate and adjudicate business in the Earth.

After you speak to your hands, speak to the land. Whatever setting God has placed you in is supposed to prosper and produce. Even if it was a wilderness before you arrived, the supernatural faith in which you operate should convert it into an oasis. So, don't criticize your location; your critiques will only steer manifestation away from it. Instead, create an atmosphere that causes you to increase in the land. Your words have the authority to implement abundance, generate economies, reduce crime, change laws, deliver kingdom concepts, empty prisons, clear out hospitals, save souls, execute justice, and transform the trajectory of entire regions. You have the power because you have the Holy Ghost and faith. Use your power to manifest the reality of heaven in your domain.

Lastly, learn to view faith as a servant, not just a substance. When the Father saved you, He transferred you from the kingdom of darkness to the kingdom of His dear Son and gave you the power to command faith as a servant. You may not know it, but the moment you believed Him, you sent faith into the light and allowed it to lead you into the place God had for you. In the same way you sent faith into the light, you can commission it to go get the wealth God has ordained for you. But you must first ensure your speech and sight are rooted in the Word of the Lord.

Hebrews 11:3 teaches that the worlds were framed by the word of God and by faith. That means faith became a servant to God's declaration and imagination. In the same manner, it will serve you if your vision and communication mirror the Word of God. Faith comes and goes by the Word and will only accomplish what you earnestly believe, so if you're not fully convinced of the Word, faith won't implement your orders. But if you're fully persuaded when you command faith to execute a task you've envisioned or spoken, it will bring resources from the unseen realm to you, its master. If all believers would garner a collective view of faith as the servant of God's people and begin to command it corporately, a massive wealth transfer would take place, the government would move by dictation of the Church, and God's kingdom would advance with lightning-like acceleration. Be one of the believers who makes that possible.

As you start to respond to faith as a God-given servant, you'll experience it as an economic force. So, speak to it as you would a dedicated assistant. Tell it to find the financial resources you need to complete your assignment and purpose, and see yourself prospering as you release that instruction. Don't be discouraged if faith seems to be delayed, and don't be distracted by unbelief. The enemy will try to turn your attention to issues and offenses sent to keep you from receiving what your servant is trying to deliver. When he does, escalate in the Word, prayer, and confession, and set your focus on the image of manifestation you've already created. Faith will return to the site of the word, so if you keep declaring it, faith will find you and manifest that which you've hoped for and God will use your supernatural stewardship to reveal His character in the Earth. As you continue to judge Him faithful and do business on His behalf, you'll realize you haven't just applied a force of faith. You've *become* one.

CONCLUSION

We've come to the end of our teaching on supernatural faith, but I believe God wants to use it as the beginning of a new supernatural life. From now on, I trust you'll live in faith every day and activate the seven forces of faith to fulfill your God-ordained purpose. That means you'll cultivate faith as a creative force and guard it with your worship and remembrance. You'll think, speak, and act like God and make your life a display of His original intent for mankind. You'll know El Emuwnah as the faithful God, and He'll always be faithful to you. His person, nature, and mind will be actively at work in you, and you'll never cease to experience His goodness and love. Through Him, you'll be filled with faith and empowered to carry out your dominion mandate.

You'll contend for the faith with supernatural strategy and see fulfillment in your household. As the Lord nourishes you and fights for your family, you'll break generational curses, access generational blessings, and transfer faith to your seed. You'll continue to grow in God, and your faith will become aman. Submission and commitment to the Lord will cause you to increase on every side, and you'll begin to see the supernatural enacted in your daily life. You'll operate in uncommon faith, initiate unusual demonstrations of power, and mature in the humility that delivers enduring influence.

You'll foster a joyful expectation that engenders miraculous change and become established in the hope that can't bring disappointment. You'll curse the spirit of nothing, decree the Word of the Lord, and produce everything ordained for your life. You'll leap from faith to faith, strength to strength, and glory to glory in the presence of God, and You'll navigate dimensions of the spirit with purpose and great precision. You'll ascend to realms that house manifestation and learn how to take residence in the supernatural. You'll craft an image of faith for every prophetic promise God has given and use your spirit, soul, and body to turn it into a tangible reality. You'll touch God with faith and remember that He's never out of your reach. You'll be easily persuaded of His Word and easily moved by His person.

You'll maximize revelation and apply faith as the currency of heaven. You'll prosper in every way as you do business for the Father, and you'll orchestrate multi-dimensional transactions that provoke supernatural invasions in the Earth. You'll stand your watch and step into portals of power, and there, God will equip you to receive, conceive, and deliver that which can come only by faith.

And now faith is coming to you. Speak to it as your servant, and command it to work on your behalf. It's ready to catapult you as a creative force, settle you as a sustaining force, fuel you as a fighting force, minister to you as a maturing force, teach you as a transformative force, confirm you as a catalytic force, and empower you as an economic force. Use each force of faith to engage your divine inheritance, and seek to live in a manner that makes the miraculous manifest in the natural. Above all else, continue to judge God faithful, refuse to waver, and get ready to soar in the supernatural. El Emuwnah will be waiting for you.

FAITH SCRIPTURES

Habakkuk 2:4
"Behold the proud, His soul is not upright in him; But the just shall live by his **faith**.

Matthew 9:22
But Jesus turned around, and when He saw her He said, "Be of good cheer, daughter; your **faith** has made you well." And the woman was made well from that hour.

Matthew 9:29
Then He touched their eyes, saying, "According to your **faith** let it be to you."

Matthew 15:28
Then Jesus answered and said to her, "O woman, great *is* your **faith**! Let it be to you as you desire." And her daughter was healed from that very hour.

Matthew 17:20
So Jesus said to them, "Because of your unbelief; for assuredly, I say to you, if you have **faith** as a mustard seed, you will say to this mountain, 'Move from here to there,' and it will move; and nothing will be impossible for you."

Matthew 21:21
So Jesus answered and said to them, "Assuredly, I say to you, if you have **faith** and do not doubt, you will not only do what was done to the fig tree, but also if you say to this mountain, 'Be removed and be cast into the sea,' it will be done."

Matthew 23:23
"Woe to you, scribes and Pharisees, hypocrites! For you pay tithe of mint and anise and cumin, and have neglected the weightier matters of the law: justice and mercy and **faith**. These you ought to have done, without leaving the others undone.

Mark 2:5
When Jesus saw their **faith**, He said to the paralytic, "Son, your sins are forgiven you."

Mark 10:52
Then Jesus said to him, "Go your way; your **faith** has made you well." And immediately he received his sight and followed Jesus on the road.

Mark 11:22
So Jesus answered and said to them, "Have **faith** in God.

Luke 7:9
When Jesus heard these things, He marveled at him, and turned around and said to the crowd that followed Him, "I say to you, I have not found such great **faith**, not even in Israel!"

Luke 7:50
Then He said to the woman, "Your **faith** has saved you. Go in peace."

Luke 8:25
But He said to them, "Where is your **faith**?" And they were afraid, and marveled, saying to one another, "Who can this be? For He commands even the winds and water, and they obey Him!"

Luke 17:5
And the apostles said to the Lord, "Increase our **faith**."

Luke 17:6
So the Lord said, "If you have **faith** as a mustard seed, you can say to this mulberry tree, 'Be pulled up by the roots and be planted in the sea,' and it would obey you.

Luke 17:19
And He said to him, "Arise, go your way. Your **faith** has made you well."

Luke 18:8
I tell you that He will avenge them speedily. Nevertheless, when the Son of Man comes, will He really find **faith** on the earth?"

Luke 18:42
Then Jesus said to him, "Receive your sight; your **faith** has made you well."

Luke 22:32
But I have prayed for you, that your **faith** should not fail; and when you have returned to *Me*, strengthen your brethren."

Acts 3:16
And His name, through **faith** in His name, has made this man strong, whom you see and know. Yes, the **faith** which *comes* through Him has given him this perfect soundness in the presence of you all.

Acts 6:7
Then the word of God spread, and the number of the disciples multiplied greatly in Jerusalem, and a great many of the priests were obedient to the **faith**.

Acts 6:8
And Stephen, full of **faith** and power, did great wonders and signs among the people.

Acts 14:9
This man heard Paul speaking. Paul, observing him intently and seeing that he had **faith** to be healed,

Acts 14:22
strengthening the souls of the disciples, exhorting *them* to continue in the **faith**, and *saying,* "We must through many tribulations enter the kingdom of God."

Acts 14:27
Now when they had come and gathered the church together, they reported all that God had done with them, and that He had opened the door of **faith** to the Gentiles.

Acts 15:9
and made no distinction between us and them, purifying their hearts by **faith**.

Acts 16:5
So the churches were strengthened in the **faith**, and increased in number daily.

Acts 26:18
to open their eyes, *in order* to turn *them* from darkness to light, and *from* the power of Satan to God, that they may receive forgiveness of sins and an inheritance among those who are sanctified by **faith** in Me.'

Romans 1:17
For in it the righteousness of God is revealed from **faith** to **faith**; as it is written, "The just shall live by **faith**."

Romans 3:22
even the righteousness of God, through **faith** in Jesus Christ, to all and on all who believe. For there is no difference;

Romans 3:25
whom God set forth *as* a propitiation by His blood, through **faith**, to demonstrate His righteousness, because in His forbearance God had passed over the sins that were previously committed,

Romans 3:26
to demonstrate at the present time His righteousness, that He might be just and the justifier of the one who has **faith** in Jesus.

Romans 3:28
Therefore we conclude that a man is justified by **faith** apart from the deeds of the law.

Romans 3:30
since *there is* one God who will justify the circumcised by **faith** and the uncircumcised through **faith**.

Romans 3:31
Do we then make void the law through **faith**? Certainly not! On the contrary, we establish the law.

Romans 4:9
Does this blessedness then *come* upon the circumcised *only,* or upon the uncircumcised also? For we say that **faith** was accounted to Abraham for righteousness.

Romans 4:11-12
And he received the sign of circumcision, a seal of the righteousness of the **faith** which *he had while still* uncircumcised, that he might be the father of all those who believe, though they are uncircumcised, that righteousness might be imputed to them also, and the father of circumcision to those who not only *are* of the circumcision, but who also walk in the steps of the **faith** which our father Abraham *had while still* uncircumcised.

Romans 4:13
For the promise that he would be the heir of the world *was* not to Abraham or to his seed through the law, but through the righteousness of **faith**.

Romans 4:16
Therefore *it is* of **faith** that *it might be* according to grace, so that the promise might be sure to all the seed, not only to those who are of the law, but also to those who are of the **faith** of Abraham, who is the father of us all

Romans 4:19
And not being weak in **faith**, he did not consider his own body, already dead (since he was about a hundred years old), and the deadness of Sarah's womb.

Romans 4:20
He did not waver at the promise of God through unbelief, but was strengthened in **faith**, giving glory to God,

Romans 5:1-2

Therefore, having been justified by **faith**, we have peace with God through our Lord Jesus Christ, through whom also we have access by **faith** into this grace in which we stand, and rejoice in hope of the glory of God.

Romans 10:8
But what does it say? "The word is near you, in your mouth and in your heart" (that's, the word of **faith** which we preach):

Romans 10:17
So then **faith** *comes* by hearing, and hearing by the word of God.

Romans 11:20
Well *said.* Because of unbelief they were broken off, and you stand by **faith**. Do not be haughty, but fear.

Romans 12:3
For I say, through the grace given to me, to everyone who is among you, not to think *of himself* more highly than he ought to think, but to think soberly, as God has dealt to each one a measure of **faith**.

Romans 12:6
Having then gifts differing according to the grace that is given to us, *let us use them:* if prophecy, *let us prophesy* in proportion to our **faith;**

Romans 14:1
Receive one who is weak in the **faith**, *but* not to disputes over doubtful things.

Romans 14:22
Do you have **faith**? Have *it* to yourself before God. Happy *is* he who does not condemn himself in what he approves.

Romans 14:23
But he who doubts is condemned if he eats, because *he* does not *eat* from **faith**; for whatever *is* not from **faith** is sin.

Romans 16:26
but now made manifest, and by the prophetic Scriptures made
known to all nations, according to the commandment of the
everlasting God, for obedience to the **faith**—

1 Corinthians 2:5
that your **faith** should not be in the wisdom of men but in the power
of God.

1 Corinthians 12:9
to another **faith** by the same Spirit, to another gifts of healings by the
same Spirit,

1 Corinthians 13:2
And though I have *the gift of* prophecy, and understand all mysteries
and all knowledge, and though I have all **faith**, so that I could
remove mountains, but have not love, I am nothing.

1 Corinthians 13:13
And now abide **faith**, hope, love, these three; but the greatest of
these *is* love.

1 Corinthians 15:14
And if Christ is not risen, then our preaching *is* empty and your **faith**
is also empty.

1 Corinthians 16:13
Watch, stand fast in the **faith**, be brave, be strong.

2 Corinthians 4:13
And since we have the same spirit of **faith**, according to what is
written, "I believed and therefore I spoke," we also believe and
therefore speak,

2 Corinthians 5:7
For we walk by **faith**, not by sight.

2 Corinthians 8:7
But as you abound in everything—in **faith**, in speech, in knowledge, in all diligence, and in your love for us—*see* that you abound in this grace also.

2 Corinthians 10:15
not boasting of things beyond measure, *that is,* in other men's labors, but having hope, *that* as your **faith** is increased, we shall be greatly enlarged by you in our sphere,

2 Corinthians 13:5
Examine yourselves *as to* whether you are in the **faith**. Test yourselves. Do you not know yourselves, that Jesus Christ is in you?—unless indeed you are disqualified.

Galatians 2:16
knowing that a man is not justified by the works of the law but by **faith** in Jesus Christ, even we have believed in Christ Jesus, that we might be justified by **faith** in Christ and not by the works of the law; for by the works of the law no flesh shall be justified.

Galatians 2:20
I have been crucified with Christ; it is no longer I who live, but Christ lives in me; and the *life* which I now live in the flesh I live by **faith** in the Son of God, who loved me and gave Himself for me.

Galatians 3:7
Therefore know that *only* those who are of **faith** are sons of Abraham.

Galatians 3:8-9
And the Scripture, foreseeing that God would justify the Gentiles by **faith**, preached the gospel to Abraham beforehand, *saying,* "In you all the nations shall be blessed. So then those who *are* of **faith** are blessed with believing Abraham.

Galatians 3:11
But that no one is justified by the law in the sight of God *is* evident, for "the just shall live by **faith**."

Galatians 3:14
that the blessing of Abraham might come upon the Gentiles in Christ
Jesus, that we might receive the promise of the Spirit through **faith**.

Galatians 3:22-23
But the Scripture has confined all under sin, that the promise by **faith**
in Jesus Christ might be given to those who believe. But before **faith**
came, we were kept under guard by the law, kept for the **faith** which
would afterward be revealed.

Galatians 3:24
Therefore the law was our tutor *to bring us* to Christ, that we might be
justified by **faith**.

Galatians 3:25
But after **faith** has come, we are no longer under a tutor.

Galatians 3:26
For you are all sons of God through **faith** in Christ Jesus.

Galatians 5:5
For we through the Spirit eagerly wait for the hope of righteousness
by **faith**.

Galatians 5:6
For in Christ Jesus neither circumcision nor uncircumcision avails
anything, but **faith** working through love.

Galatians 6:10
Therefore, as we have opportunity, let us do good to all, especially to
those who are of the household of **faith**.

Ephesians 2:8
For by grace you have been saved through **faith**, and that not of
yourselves; *it is* the gift of God,

Ephesians 3:12
in whom we have boldness and access with confidence through **faith** in Him.

Ephesians 3:17
that Christ may dwell in your hearts through **faith**; that you, being rooted and grounded in love,

Ephesians 4:5
one Lord, one **faith**, one baptism;

Ephesians 6:16
above all, taking the shield of **faith** with which you will be able to quench all the fiery darts of the wicked one.

Philippians 1:27
Only let your conduct be worthy of the gospel of Christ, so that whether I come and see you or am absent, I may hear of your affairs, that you stand fast in one spirit, with one mind striving together for the **faith** of the gospel,

Philippians 3:9
and be found in Him, not having my own righteousness, which *is* from the law, but that which *is* through **faith** in Christ, the righteousness which is from God by **faith**;

Colossians 2:5
For though I am absent in the flesh, yet I am with you in spirit, rejoicing to see your *good* order and the steadfastness of your **faith** in Christ.

Colossians 2:7
rooted and built up in Him and established in the **faith**, as you have been taught, abounding in it with thanksgiving.

Colossians 2:12
buried with Him in baptism, in which you also were raised with *Him* through **faith** in the working of God, who raised Him from the dead.

1 Thessalonians 1:3
remembering without ceasing your work of **faith**, labor of love, and patience of hope in our Lord Jesus Christ in the sight of our God and Father,

1 Thessalonians 3:7
therefore, brethren, in all our affliction and distress we were comforted concerning you by your **faith**.

1 Thessalonians 5:8
But let us who are of the day be sober, putting on the breastplate of **faith** and love, and *as* a helmet the hope of salvation.

2 Thessalonians 1:3-4
We are bound to thank God always for you, brethren, as it is fitting, because your **faith** grows exceedingly, and the love of every one of you all abounds toward each other, so that we ourselves boast of you among the churches of God for your patience and **faith** in all your persecutions and tribulations that you endure,

2 Thessalonians 1:11
Therefore we also pray always for you that our God would count you worthy of *this* calling, and fulfill all the good pleasure of *His* goodness and the work of **faith** with power,

1 Timothy 1:5
Now the purpose of the commandment is love from a pure heart, *from* a good conscience, and *from* sincere **faith**,

1 Timothy 1:14
And the grace of our Lord was exceedingly abundant, with **faith** and love which are in Christ Jesus.

1 Timothy 3:9
holding the mystery of the **faith** with a pure conscience.

1 Timothy 4:6
If you instruct the brethren in these things, you will be a good minister of Jesus Christ, nourished in the words of **faith** and of the good doctrine which you have carefully followed.

1 Timothy 4:12
Let no one despise your youth, but be an example to the believers in word, in conduct, in love, in spirit, in **faith**, in purity.

1 Timothy 6:11
But you, O man of God, flee these things and pursue righteousness, godliness, **faith**, love, patience, gentleness.

1 Timothy 6:12
Fight the good fight of **faith**, lay hold on eternal life, to which you were also called and have confessed the good confession in the presence of many witnesses.

2 Timothy 1:13
Hold fast the pattern of sound words which you have heard from me, in **faith** and love which are in Christ Jesus.

2 Timothy 2:22
Flee also youthful lusts; but pursue righteousness, **faith**, love, peace with those who call on the Lord out of a pure heart.

2 Timothy 4:7
I have fought the good fight, I have finished the race, I have kept the **faith**.

Hebrews 4:2
For indeed the gospel was preached to us as well as to them; but the word which they heard did not profit them, not being mixed with **faith** in those who heard *it*.

Hebrews 6:12
that you do not become sluggish, but imitate those who through **faith** and patience inherit the promises.

Hebrews 10:22
let us draw near with a true heart in full assurance of **faith**, having our hearts sprinkled from an evil conscience and our bodies washed with pure water.

Hebrews 10:38
Now the just shall live by **faith**; But if *anyone* draws back, My soul has no pleasure in him."

Hebrews 11:1
Now **faith** is the substance of things hoped for, the evidence of things not seen.

Hebrews 11:3
By **faith** we understand that the worlds were framed by the word of God, so that the things which are seen were not made of things which are visible.

Hebrews 11:6
But without **faith** *it is* impossible to please *Him,* for he who comes to God must believe that He is, and *that* He is a rewarder of those who diligently seek Him.

Hebrews 11:8-9
By **faith** Abraham obeyed when he was called to go out to the place which he would receive as an inheritance. And he went out, not knowing where he was going. By **faith** he dwelt in the land of promise as *in* a foreign country, dwelling in tents with Isaac and Jacob, the heirs with him of the same promise;

Hebrews 11:11
By **faith** Sarah herself also received strength to conceive seed, and she bore a child when she was past the age, because she judged Him **faith**ful who had promised.

Hebrews 11:21
By **faith** Jacob, when he was dying, blessed each of the sons of Joseph, and worshiped, *leaning* on the top of his staff.

Hebrews 11:29
By **faith** they passed through the Red Sea as by dry *land, whereas* the Egyptians, attempting to do so, were drowned.

Hebrews 11:30
By **faith** the walls of Jericho fell down after they were encircled for seven days.

Hebrews 12:2
looking unto Jesus, the author and finisher of *our* **faith**, who for the joy that was set before Him endured the cross, despising the shame, and has sat down at the right hand of the throne of God.

Hebrews 13:7
Remember those who rule over you, who have spoken the word of God to you, whose **faith** follow, considering the outcome of *their* conduct.

James 1:3
knowing that the testing of your **faith** produces patience.

James 1:6
But let him ask in **faith**, with no doubting, for he who doubts is like a wave of the sea driven and tossed by the wind.

James 2:5
Listen, my beloved brethren: Has God not chosen the poor of this world *to be* rich in **faith** and heirs of the kingdom which He promised to those who love Him?

James 2:26
For as the body without the spirit is dead, so **faith** without works is dead also.

James 5:15
And the prayer of **faith** will save the sick, and the Lord will raise him up. And if he has committed sins, he will be forgiven.

1 Peter 1:5
who are kept by the power of God through **faith** for salvation ready to be revealed in the last time.

1 Peter 1:7
that the genuineness of your **faith**, *being* much more precious than gold that perishes, though it is tested by fire, may be found to praise, honor, and glory at the revelation of Jesus Christ,

1 Peter 1:21
who through Him believe in God, who raised Him from the dead and gave Him glory, so that your **faith** and hope are in God.

2 Peter 1:1
Simon Peter, a bondservant and apostle of Jesus Christ, To those who have obtained like precious **faith** with us by the righteousness of our God and Savior Jesus Christ:

2 Peter 1:5
But also for this very reason, giving all diligence, add to your **faith** virtue, to virtue knowledge,

1 John 5:4
For whatever is born of God overcomes the world. And this is the victory that has overcome the world—our **faith**.

Jude 1:3
Beloved, while I was very diligent to write to you concerning our common salvation, I found it necessary to write to you exhorting you to contend earnestly for the **faith** which was once for all delivered to the saints.

Jude 1:20
But you, beloved, building yourselves up on your most holy **faith**, praying in the Holy Spirit,

Revelation 2:19
"I know your works, love, service, **faith**, and your patience; and *as* for your works, the last *are* more than the first.

Revelation 14:12
Here is the patience of the saints; here *are* those who keep the commandments of God and the **faith** of Jesus.

Genesis 15:6
And he **believe**d in the Lord, and He accounted it to him for righteousness.

Exodus 4:31
So the people **believe**d; and when they heard that the Lord had visited the children of Israel and that He had looked on their affliction, then they bowed their heads and worshiped.

2 Chronicles 20:20
So they rose early in the morning and went out into the Wilderness of Tekoa; and as they went out, Jehoshaphat stood and said, "Hear me, O Judah and you inhabitants of Jerusalem: **Believe** in the Lord your God, and you shall be established; **believe** His prophets, and you shall prosper."

Psalm 27:13
I would have lost heart, unless I had **believe**d That I would see the goodness of the Lord In the land of the living.

Isaiah 7:9
The head of Ephraim *is* Samaria, And the head of Samaria *is* Remaliah's son. If you will not **believe**, Surely you shall not be established." ' "

Matthew 8:13
Then Jesus said to the centurion, "Go your way; and as you have **believe**d, *so* let it be done for you." And his servant was healed that same hour.

Mark 9:23
Jesus said to him, "If you can **believe**, all things *are* possible to him who **believe**s."

Mark 11:23
For assuredly, I say to you, whoever says to this mountain, 'Be removed and be cast into the sea,' and does not doubt in his heart, but **believe**s that those things he says will be done, he will have whatever he says.

Mark 11:24
Therefore I say to you, whatever things you ask when you pray, **believe** that you receive *them*, and you will have *them*.

Mark 16:17
And these signs will follow those who **believe**: In My name they will cast out demons; they will speak with new tongues;

Luke 1:45
Blessed *is* she who **believe**d, for there will be a fulfillment of those things which were told her from the Lord."

Luke 8:50
But when Jesus heard *it*, He answered him, saying, "Do not be afraid; only **believe**, and she will be made well."

John 1:12
But as many as received Him, to them He gave the right to become children of God, to those who **believe** in His name:

John 3:16
For God so loved the world that He gave His only begotten Son, that whoever **believe**s in Him should not perish but have everlasting life.

John 6:35
And Jesus said to them, "I am the bread of life. He who comes to Me shall never hunger, and he who **believe**s in Me shall never thirst.

John 6:47
Most assuredly, I say to you, he who **believe**s in Me has everlasting life.

John 7:38
He who **believe**s in Me, as the Scripture has said, out of his heart will flow rivers of living water."

John 9:38
Then he said, "Lord, I **believe**!" And he worshiped Him.

John 11:25
Jesus said to her, "I am the resurrection and the life. He who **believe**s in Me, though he may die, he shall live.

John 14:1
"Let not your heart be troubled; you **believe** in God, **believe** also in Me.

John 14:11
Believe Me that I *am* in the Father and the Father in Me, or else **believe** Me for the sake of the works themselves.

John 14:12
"Most assuredly, I say to you, he who **believe**s in Me, the works that I do he will do also; and greater *works* than these he will do, because I go to My Father.

John 17:20
"I do not pray for these alone, but also for those who will **believe** in Me through their word;

Acts 8:37
Then Philip said, "If you **believe** with all your heart, you may." And he answered and said, "I **believe** that Jesus Christ is the Son of God."

Romans 1:16
For I am not ashamed of the gospel of Christ, for it is the power of God to salvation for everyone who **believe**s, for the Jew first and also for the Greek.

Romans 10:9
that if you confess with your mouth the Lord Jesus and **believe** in
your heart that God has raised Him from the dead, you will be saved.

Romans 10:10
For with the heart one **believe**s unto righteousness, and with the
mouth confession is made unto salvation.

2 Corinthians 4:13
And since we have the same spirit of faith, according to what is
written, "I **believe**d and therefore I spoke," we also **believe** and
therefore speak,

Ephesians 1:19
and what *is* the exceeding greatness of His power toward us who
believe, according to the working of His mighty power

2 Timothy 1:12
For this reason I also suffer these things; nevertheless I am not
ashamed, for I know whom I have **believe**d and am persuaded that
He is able to keep what I have committed to Him until that Day.

Hebrews 4:3
For we who have **believe**d do enter that rest, as He has said: "So I
swore in My wrath, 'They shall not enter My rest,' " although the
works were finished from the foundation of the world.

Hebrews 10:39
But we are not of those who draw back to perdition, but of those
who **believe** to the saving of the soul.

1 John 5:5
Who is he who overcomes the world, but he who **believe**s that Jesus
is the Son of God?

1 John 5:13
These things I have written to you who **believe** in the name of the
Son of God, that you may know that you have eternal life, and that
you may *continue to* **believe** in the name of the Son of God.

2 Samuel 22:31
As for God, His way *is* perfect; The word of the Lord *is* proven; He *is* a shield to all who **trust** in Him.

Job 13:15
Though He slay me, yet will I **trust** Him. Even so, I will defend my own ways before Him.

Psalm 2:12
Kiss the Son, lest He be angry, And you perish *in* the way, When His wrath is kindled but a little. Blessed *are* all those who put their **trust** in Him.

Psalm 4:5
Offer the sacrifices of righteousness, And put your **trust** in the Lord.

Psalm 18:2
The Lord is my rock and my fortress and my deliverer; My God, my strength, in whom I will **trust**; My shield and the horn of my salvation, my stronghold.

Psalm 20:7
Some *trust* in chariots, and some in horses; But we will remember the name of the Lord our God.

Psalm 25:2
O my God, I **trust** in You; Let me not be ashamed; Let not my enemies triumph over me.

Psalm 31:1
In You, O Lord, I put my **trust**; Let me never be ashamed; Deliver me in Your righteousness.

Psalm 34:8
Oh, taste and see that the Lord *is* good; Blessed *is* the man *who* **trust**s in Him!

Psalm 37:3
Trust in the Lord, and do good; Dwell in the land, and feed on His faithfulness.

Psalm 37:5
Commit your way to the Lord, **Trust** also in Him, And He shall bring *it* to pass.

Psalm 56:3
Whenever I am afraid, I will **trust** in You.

Psalm 56:4
In God (I will praise His word), In God I have put my **trust**; I will not fear. What can flesh do to me?

Psalm 62:8
Trust in Him at all times, you people; Pour out your heart before Him; God *is* a refuge for us. *Selah*

Psalm 91:2
I will say of the Lord, "*He is* my refuge and my fortress; My God, in Him I will **trust**."

Psalm 115:11
You who fear the Lord, **trust** in the Lord; He *is* their help and their shield.

Psalm 118:8
It is better to **trust** in the Lord Than to put confidence in man.

Psalm 125:1
Those who **trust** in the Lord *Are* like Mount Zion, *Which* cannot be moved, *but* abides forever.

Proverbs 3:5
Trust in the Lord with all your heart, And lean not on your own understanding;

Proverbs 29:25
The fear of man brings a snare, But whoever **trust**s in the Lord shall be safe.

Proverbs 30:5
Every word of God *is* pure; He *is* a shield to those who put their **trust** in Him.

Isaiah 12:2
Behold, God *is* my salvation, I will **trust** and not be afraid; 'For Yah, the Lord, *is* my strength and song; He also has become my salvation.'

Isaiah 26:3
you'll keep *him* in perfect peace, *Whose* mind *is* stayed *on You*, Because he **trust**s in You.

Isaiah 26:4
Trust in the Lord forever, For in Yah, the Lord, *is* everlasting strength.

Isaiah 50:10
"Who among you fears the Lord? Who obeys the voice of His Servant? Who walks in darkness And has no light? Let him **trust** in the name of the Lord And rely upon his God.

Jeremiah 17:5
Thus says the Lord: "Cursed *is* the man who **trust**s in man And makes flesh his strength, Whose heart departs from the Lord.

Jeremiah 17:7
"Blessed *is* the man who **trust**s in the Lord, And whose hope is the Lord.

Nahum 1:7
The Lord *is* good, A stronghold in the day of trouble; And He knows those who **trust** in Him.

Ephesians 1:13
In Him you also *trusted*, after you heard the word of truth, the gospel of your salvation; in whom also, having believed, you were sealed with the Holy Spirit of promise,

1 Timothy 4:10
For to this *end* we both labor and suffer reproach, because we **trust** in the living God, who is *the* Savior of all men, especially of those who believe.

Hebrews 2:13
And again: "I will put My **trust** in Him." And again: "Here am I and the children whom God has given Me."

SOURCES CONSULTED

"Amar." Accessed February 16, 2019.
https://biblehub.com/hebrew/559.htm.

"Azotus." Accessed March 2, 2019.
https://biblehub.com/topical/a/ashdod_or_azotus.htm.

"Dominion." Accessed March 11, 2019.
https://www.dictionary.com/browse/dominion.

"Elpis." Accessed January 28, 2019.
https://www.blueletterbible.org/lang/lexicon/lexicon.cfm?strongs=G1680.

"Energy." Accessed February 8, 2019.
https://www.dictionary.com/browse/energy.

"Epi." Accessed March 6, 2019.
https://biblehub.com/greek/1909.htm.

Fox, Eddie H. and George E. Morris. *The Faith-Sharing New Testament with the Psalms.* Nashville: Cokesbury, 1996.

Holladay, William L., ed. *A Concise Hebrew and Aramaic Lexicon of the Old Testament.* Grand Rapids: Eerdmans, 1988.

Nesbitt, Sharon R. *Chosen for Greatness: Discovering your Dominion Mandate.* Travelers Rest, SC: True Potential Publishing, 2013.

Nesbitt, Sharon R. *Scarlet Stream: Unveiling the Mystery: Releasing the Supernatural.* 2015.

"Pistis." Accessed January 21, 2019.
https://www.blueletterbible.org/lang/lexicon/lexicon.cfm?strongs=G4102.

Strong, James. *The Strongest Strong's Exhaustive Concordance of the Bible.* Grand Rapids: Zondervan, 2001.

Trafton, Anne. "In the Blink of An Eye: MIT Neuroscientists Find the Brain Can Identify Images Seen for As Little As 13 Milliseconds." Accessed March 4, 2019. http://news.mit.edu/2014/in-the-blink-of-an-eye-0116.

World's Reference Library. *World's Concise Bible Concordance.* Nashville: World Publishing, 2004.

ABOUT
DR. SHARON NESBITT

Dr. Sharon Nesbitt is the founding Pastor of Dominion World Outreach Ministries, a multi-racial, non-denominational ministry located in Marion, AR. She is a coveted spiritual leader, philanthropist, author and humanitarian. She has dedicated her life to making this world a better place. Her goal is to positively impact and transform communities both locally and globally by leaving a legacy of hope, morality and ethics to the next generation.

Dr. Nesbitt motivates and inspires people to reach beyond cultural and socioeconomic barriers. Her sensitivity to the needs of people and vision to minister to the nations prompted the founding of several organizations to include Dominion World Development Corporation and Dominion Bible School in Guatemala City. Dr. Nesbitt has a passion for young people and endeavors to see that no child is left behind regardless of race, creed or color. Additionally, she has a heart for those who are incarcerated and has partnered with prisons to break the cycle of recidivism. She believes that prison reform is necessary to ensure human rights are protected and prospects for social reintegration are increased.

Dr. Nesbitt has authored many books and bible studies which includes her best sellers, Chosen for Greatness and Scarlet Stream. Additionally, Dr. Nesbitt's entrepreneurial anointing has led and directed the acquisition and development of land and facilities on behalf of the ministry. The most recent purchase of 52 acres of land will house the new Dominion campus.

She is the proud mother of two and grandmother of two. She has an uncanny ability to reach people of all ages and backgrounds, inspiring believers the world over to operate in new levels of faith.

ADDITIONAL RESOURCES FROM DR. NESBITT

- *Chosen for Greatness: Discovering your Dominion Mandate*

- *Scarlet Stream: Unveiling the Mystery: Releasing the Supernatural*

- *Seeds: Daily Decrees that Bring Dominion*

- *Seeds for Divine Health: Daily Decrees that Bring Dominion*

- *Seeds for Covenant Wealth: Daily Decrees that Bring Dominion*

CONTACT INFORMATION

Sharon R. Nesbitt Ministries

P.O. Box 41

Marion, AR 72364

Phone: (870) 739-1331

Fax: (870) 739-1332

Toll Free: (866) 579-5807

Email: info@dominionworld.org

www.dominionworld.org

NOTES

[1] "Energy," accessed February 8, 2019. https://www.dictionary.com/browse/energy.

[2] James Strong. *The Strongest Strong's Exhaustive Concordance of the Bible* (Grand Rapids: Zondervan, 2001), 1361.

[3] "Amar," accessed February 16, 2019. https://biblehub.com/hebrew/559.htm.

[4] James Strong. *The Strongest Strong's Exhaustive Concordance of the Bible*, 1362.

[5] Ibid, 1361.

[6] "Dominion," accessed March 11, 2019. https://www.dictionary.com/browse/dominion.

[7] Ibid.

[8] Sharon R. Nesbitt. *Chosen for Greatness: Discovering Your Dominion Mandate* (Travelers Rest, SC: True Potential Publishing, 2013) 22.

[9] James Strong. *The Strongest Strong's Exhaustive Concordance of the Bible*, 1361.

[10] For further study on the role of *aman* as an establishing agent, see Isaiah 7:9, "If ye won't believe (aman), surely ye shall not be established (addition mine)."

[11] "Elpis," accessed January 28, 2019. https://www.blueletterbible.org/lang/lexicon/lexicon.cfm?strongs=G1680.

[12] On the statement "when something that God created can't be identified, confusion enters the land," I do not mean to suggest that *everyone* has to rightly identify the creation. But someone should be able to do so. (Even Jesus, the firstborn of all creation, was rightly identified by Peter, who proclaimed that He was the Messiah.)

[13] "Epi," accessed March 6, 2019. https://biblehub.com/greek/1909.htm.

[14] Sharon R. Nesbitt. *Scarlet Stream: Unveiling the Mystery: Releasing the Supernatural*, 53.

[15] Ibid, 61.

[16] James Strong. *The Strongest Strong's Exhaustive Concordance of the Bible*, 1525.

[17] "Pistis," accessed January 21, 2019.
https://www.blueletterbible.org/lang/lexicon/lexicon.cfm?strongs=G4102.

[18] Azotus was the Greek name given to the city known as Ashdod to the Hebrews. "Azotus," accessed March 2, 2019. https://biblehub.com/topical/a/ashdod_or_azotus.htm.

[19] This account also appears in Mark 5 and Luke 9, with slight variations in each telling.

[20] Anne Trafton. "In the Blink of An Eye: MIT Neuroscientists Find the Brain Can Identify Images Seen for As Little As 13 Milliseconds," accessed March 4, 2019. http://news.mit.edu/2014/in-the-blink-of-an-eye-0116.

[21] Other scriptures that underscore God's faithfulness include 1 Cor. 10:13, 2 Thess. 3:3, and 1 Thess. 5:24.

[22] James Strong. *The Strongest Strong's Exhaustive Concordance of the Bible*, 1492.